_ JNTENTS

- Develop an awareness of others

- Develop the right attitude

- Learn about your image

- Learn simplicity

Preparation • Arrival • During the Meeting • Time • Goodwill concessions or toughness • Negotiating Overseas

- Risk assessment considerations

- Risk management methods

PART 2 – EVENTS

Good management of risk means success • The human factor • Communication • Objectives • Internal Company Procedures • After Contract Award, Be Proactive

Think "loss", not "profit" • Understand what you are agreeing to • Share risk : Pricing, Insuring, Avoiding, Containing, Sharing • Limit Liability • Exclude liability for risks where the potential loss cannot be assessed • Don't "bet" the Company on any single contract or group of contracts

Sense Advisory Instructions • Strategic Planning

- Reducing the Risk of Dispute Resolution

Choice of Governing Law • Key contractual provisions dealing with dispute resolution • Arbitration versus Litigation • Use of Arbitration • Arbitration and the New York Convention of 1958 • Alternative Dispute Resolution and Expert Determination • Risk Allocation in Contracts • Conduct of the Parties during Dispute Resolution

- The attitude/approach of the developer/buyer is critical

- Risk spectrum

- Buyer realism

- Contractor self-preservation methods

Never accept a "take it or leave it" approach by the Buyer • Know the bottom line • Monitor carefully Buyer requests and decision-making after contract award • Pay attention to record keeping • Specify clearly the conditions applicable to bank bonds and performance guarantees • Exclude liability for economic or consequential loss • Be clear about what liability is accepted for delays to a project • Be clear about what documents are required to complete a project • Define clearly the Scope of Work • Cash flow, currency and material pricing fluctuations

- **The foreseeability test and soils/ground conditions**

- **Contractors: the final word**

PART 3

PART 1: PEOPLE

CHAPTER 1

INTRODUCTION – PEOPLE RISK

How life treats you, how much of a success or failure you are in your personal life, will depend on how you deal with the impact of people and events, and the risks they bring. It is the same in business life. Personal life and business life are inter-linked. They both depend on how the risk associated with people and events is handled day to day.

Risk needs managing. How you deal with risk will dictate whether success or failure comes your way.

The spectacular collapse of many well-known businesses over recent years has been a direct result of human frailties in a way never before witnessed. These collapses have caused devastation to employees and communities. The way *people act* affects the fortunes of a business.

Setting out simple rules that can be followed by everyone will help to reduce the impact, or risk, of people's actions and increase the prospect of success. People make or break businesses by their conduct. Management and reduction of the risk caused by the way people think and act ("people risk") is therefore as important to the success of a business as the failure to manage traditional commercial risks effectively.

The risks caused by *people's actions* and *events* are of equal importance, and the way they are handled will dictate the fortunes of a company. It is rare for *events* on their own to cause a company to fail: it is far more likely that the way an event is dealt with by *people* will have the most critical effect on fortunes.

Reducing risk should be simple and easy to follow. The first part of this book provides easy-to-follow guidelines for reducing adverse impacts and risk, and for achieving success through the way people conduct themselves.

Your personal "traits", in other words the distinguishing features or characteristics of your personal nature, will dictate what happens to you in life. They will lead you to success or failure, comfort or poverty, companionship or loneliness.

These traits are so important that they affect the conduct, and success or failure, of businesses. Put another way, *you,* rather than the circumstances that you have to deal with on a daily basis, will affect the fortunes of the business you work in.

The critical personal issues which will be discussed in achieving success and which are fundamental to the reduction of adverse impacts and excessive risk taking are summarized below:

- **Overinflated ego**: This will ultimately limit or block your progress and success in life;
- **Good working environment**: This is not going to exist if the dominant features of the way a business is run are fear, worry, secrecy, and lack of communication;
- **Greed and selfishness**: These traits are

epitomized by reckless profit seeking and the desire to override the checks and balances built into a business, which leads to business failure;
- **Complacency**: Success breeds complacency. Staying focused, observing and listening to what is going on around you is crucial;
- **Observing, Listening, and Patience**: These practices are the keys to success. Environments that limit constructive feedback also limit opportunity;
- **Change**: Change occurs in life. Nothing stays the same. How a company manages changed conditions will influence the level of success or failure;
- **Get to know yourself**: Top class meeting and negotiation skills cannot be exhibited until you know your own strengths and weaknesses;
- **Get to know those you are doing business with**: Being aware of the strengths and weaknesses of others is crucial to your success or failure;
- **Awareness**: Awareness of others reduces risk and creates success. This requires three skills: observation, listening, and patience. Through these skills you learn all the information you need;
- **Attitude**: Develop the right attitude. Positive people attract success and negative people attract failure;
- **Image**: Create the right image. Image matters.
- **Simplicity**: Keep things simple. Simplicity creates clarity. Clarity creates good business deals.

Long term success cannot be achieved without practical rules that people can live by.

The management and control of people's actions is a far more subtle art than the process of managing commercial risk, as we can see from lurid media coverage of recent catastrophic business failures. Losses, failure and chaotic, unproductive or unhappy working environments are avoidable, or their impact can be reduced. This book will tell you how this can be done.

Many companies have very sophisticated procedures in place to manage commercial risk and the impact that the occurrence of adverse events may have on their business, but what about the risk caused by people? We need to make sure this is addressed as thoroughly as we would attend to commercial risk.

We never grow tired of hearing stories concerning the downfall of people with inflated egos, greed and arrogance, and lately there has been no shortage of extraordinarily good examples.

In providing guidelines on conduct in business, the influence of negative human traits on business performance will be analysed, and the reasons why negative characteristics can cause a company to fail.

Conversely, performance can be influenced beneficially by certain positive human traits. The guidelines will show specific ways that people can conduct themselves with others to reduce the chance of failure, whether they are running a company or negotiating deals.

In the foreign market, awareness of unfair and corrupt practices should not be underestimated for both personal and corporate wellbeing, and guidelines for combating this threat are provided.

Practical guidelines to reduce commercial risk are set out in the second part of the book. Good management of the impact of events in commerce and industry brings success. Understanding the key risk principles, the words that can hurt your company in documents, understanding how to allocate risk in deals, how to operate in foreign markets, and how to reduce risk when settling disputes, are vital. If a matter has become overly complicated, it is probably going wrong.

Throughout this book the words "corporation", "company" and "organization" will be used interchangeably, as the case requires, and in the context of this book, it is not intended that they should be viewed differently. Explanation is also due to women readers who will note the use of the masculine gender throughout. This is purely for ease of reference, and the reference to a person as "he" can equally mean "she".

The goal we are driving towards in this book is business success.

This goal requires greater focus on *people's conduct* so that failure is reduced.

It also requires an understanding of how to work with risk so that the impact of people and events can be utilized to become a feature of the success of a business.

By understanding and actually putting into practice the principles set out in this book, your business can be transformed and long term success achieved.

Success should be a simple process. The best solutions are always simple, as we shall see.

CHAPTER 2

NEGATIVE HUMAN TRAITS

Could you envisage a world without risk? What would a world without risk look like? A world without lawyers? Where businessmen trusted each other?

That world is rarely encountered in our current lives, but it would be a world where trust reigned supreme. It would also be a world, long forgotten, where two of the most important words on earth were used more regularly, even in a business context: the words 'love' and 'gratitude'. At first glance, these words sound incredibly out of place when applied to "business". In three decades on the front line of commerce and industry they were not words that I heard very often. In the context of doing business however, they refer to your conduct towards others and acknowledging the contribution of others. Attitude and awareness are critical to lasting business success, as this book will reveal.

Somewhere in the dim and distant past, these two words, love and gratitude, were the words which the world's religions were supposedly founded on. If these words were still at the forefront of everyone's daily lives, business and personal, then there would be no need for laws; we would trust each other and not worry about the fine print of a contract.

That day may come, but until then, we must continue to exist in a less idyllic world where precaution is required in our dealings.

So let's return to today's reality: there are certain key human traits we encounter in our daily lives which will either increase or decrease the risks we encounter depending on which traits are most dominant. These are negative traits and positive traits.

Negative traits, which can break businesses, are: inflated ego, arrogance, selfishness, greed, fear, worry, hatred, anger. Positive traits, which can help to make a business a success, are: awareness (or "mindfulness"), care and thoughtfulness. You might think that the positive traits appear lightweight, and therefore lacking in power and importance, but this is not the case. They are the opposite of the negative traits, so produce the opposite effect to the negative traits. This produces power. This will become apparent to you as you read on.

Before analyzing negative and positive human traits and their effect on our fortunes, it is worth putting them in the context of our everyday lives. The way you think directly affects the life you are living and your success in business. We underestimate the power of thought. Your thoughts actually "create" the world around you, the people that you live with and associate with, your material status, and consequently your happiness, and the happiness of those around you.

It is not unusual for people to spend most of their lives trapped by society and unable to see beyond the everyday process of survival. People finish school, find a job, get married, have kids, and struggle day to day to create a comfortable home existence. This takes all our thoughts and energies (and is what society expects). Then, at the end of our lives, when it is all behind us, we look back over our lives and say to ourselves, "was that it"? "Was that all"?

Do you ever stop and think what you are doing with your life? Whether you have a plan? What might make you happier? Perhaps you think about what you will do when you retire, or when you cash in the wealth that you hope to have created? Do you believe that material success will make you happy, yet somehow as you get to a certain level of wealth you still don't really get any feeling of joy or take pleasure in the life you are leading?

The truth is that deep inside you, everyone knows what makes them happy. It's just that most people don't listen to the thoughts inside them, their inner feelings, their inner voice talking to them if they were ever to stop for one second and listen carefully. Instead, they listen to their "ego", not their "instinct", and this leads them down paths that are not necessarily aligned with their "true self". This makes them unhappy, or unfulfilled. This affects business.

Ego

"Ego" is a natural part of everyone's psyche, and vital for success, and contributes to self-confidence, optimism and success. But uncontrolled, overinflated ego is one of the biggest contributors to poor management performance. Many commentators have singled out "ego", the misuse of ego, as the biggest single factor in corporate losses. We cannot simply "dispose" of our ego if we operate in the corporate world, where serious competition exists and peace and quiet is hard to find, so we must learn to use our ego in a positive way.

Ego feeds off how the world thinks about you, and how you see your image in the world. Ego is very powerful and will always override instinct, your spirit deep inside, unless you constantly listen to what the instinct is saying through the overpowering noise of your ego.

How you deal with your ego will dictate a lot about your success, happiness, approval rating, and friendships in life. The truth is that you can be whatever you want to be, if you, rather than your ego, are in control of your life. Or rather, you can become your "True Self", which is, of course, a magnificent person.

When a person has an overinflated ego, he cannot ultimately go far. If he achieves some level of success, it won't be for long. The main reason is that he cannot sustain the cooperation of those around him for long. He is going to be an unpleasant person to work with, because he is thinking of himself too much, and is not going to be listening to others. He may even interrupt or cut short someone else's speech or conversation. What those people don't realize is that the way people act doesn't go unnoticed, and it drives away career advancements and relationships. An uncontrolled, overinflated ego is a description that most people will not admit to having, but it's not difficult for those around you to feel the air of arrogance, pride, inflexibility and sense of superiority.

How you conduct yourself with others affects the risk in doing business, and the performance of that business, and later on in this book we will look in more detail at ways you should conduct yourself with others to reduce risk and increase performance. Firstly however, the key factors that affect performance are summarized below.

The impact of ego affects happiness. Progress in life can be measured by your level of happiness. You think differently when you are happy. Ego is responsible for negative traits which can make life a misery. You cannot be happy if you allow negative traits to dominate your everyday life. And success is not related to how happy you are, because you can be successful and unhappy.

Your ability to achieve long term business success or happiness is dependent on having control over your ego, and this will not be the case if you are guilty of exhibiting any of the following negative human traits:

- **Fear**

How many people work in an unhappy working environment, where people are driven by fear of failure rather than the joy of success? Where the possibility of being humiliated is common and the chances of someone encouraging you, saying "well done" or "thank you" is rarely or never heard? Fear of failure starts at the top of an organization. You know an organization is not a "people" business when you discover that staff turnover is high, morale is low, productivity is low, and sick days taken are high. When individuals are more interested in personal glory or gain rather than those around them or the organization as a whole, the business ultimately suffers. Every member of an organization should feel that the organization as a whole matters, and that they as an individual within that organization are as important as everyone else. Morale and productivity isn't going to be helped when you see the top guys getting all the perks and benefits with those in the middle or at the bottom being left underpaid, unrecognized and frustrated.

Fear of failure, or fear of making a mistake, isn't going to help you or your company. Many people have created 'glass ceilings' in their lives because they have failed in some task in the past, and haven't let go of the failure.

"Glass ceilings" are invisible barriers which impede our advancement either through limitations we place on ourselves, or limitations we allow others to place on us.

Sometimes to move forwards we must let go of the past. We've all made mistakes, and regardless of whether you were lucky enough to put the mistake right, as long as we have learnt from the mistake and let it go, nothing more can be asked of you. The losses, the failures, the mistakes you make, are part of living, the journey we are on, and we are unlikely to find success without having tasted and accepted failure. It's not failing that is the problem, it's the way you deal with it.

So how should you go about letting go of the past, things from your past that are holding you back? Simply by acknowledging them and letting them go. Later in the book we will look at "conduct" in more detail (because it affects your business) but remember this right now: your thoughts will influence your present and future, as they did your past. So, incredible though it seems, by simply saying to yourself words such as "I am no longer affected by [the event], I am letting go of [the event from] the past", you are already on the way to a better future, because your thoughts will change the way you act and perform. Every time you say "I can't", you really won't.

- **Worry**

One of the features of worrying is that it destroys our ability to concentrate. When we worry, our minds jump here there and everywhere and we lose our clarity of mind and the power of decision.

Next time you start worrying, which won't be long away, why not stop for a minute and instead of worrying, be constructive. Think this way: what is the worst thing that could happen as a result of the problem or failure? Once you have worked this out, which invariably isn't as bad as you think, reconcile yourself to accepting it. From then on, devote your time and energy to trying to improve on the worst that could happen.

This short formula will allow you to concentrate and reach a satisfactory outcome. The formula works just as well in your domestic life as your corporate life. Once you have accepted the worst case scenario, you have nothing more to lose, and can concentrate on achieving something better than your worst. That's freedom of thought isn't it? So maybe you thought you'd make more money than you did, or maybe you lost more than you expected, or the project is going to take more time than you thought, but you know where you stand, the bottom line, and it won't be as bad as you thought. Why? Because you know what the worst case scenario is, and certainty is a relief. Fear and worry need to be contained for peace of mind.

So you think you've got a problem and you're worrying about it: get the facts first before you start worrying. Most of the worries we have are caused by trying to make decisions before we have sufficient knowledge on which to base a decision. Mostly, we focus on facts which support what we already think, and this is where the worry starts, because we are not being realistic, impartial, objective, and keeping our emotions out of our thinking. We must address all the facts before we jump to a conclusion.

Start your problem solving (and worry reduction) by getting the facts and defining what the problem is. Once you have all the facts, you can better analyze the cause of the problem. You can then consider the appropriate solution to the problem and commence the remedy.

Finally, there is an expression in English Law which says "the law does not concern itself with trifles", the Latin expression being "De minimis non curat lex". If a triviality is unworthy of the law's attention, you should think about the impact of trivialities in your life too. How often have you wasted time, energy and emotion over something which, if you stopped to think about it for a second, you would realize was just trivial, and of no real concern. If the law won't support trivial or frivolous actions by one person against another, *you* must stop worrying about them too and get on with using your valuable time in a positive productive way. Why not say to yourself: "how much does this thing I'm worrying about really matter to me?" At what point should you simply decide to forget it and close the matter? Time is money, or valuable at least, and you must always think how much time the matter has irrationally taken from your life.

- **Hatred and Anger**

There is always a high price that you pay for getting even. Look at things from the point of view of someone you consider your "enemy" or "competitor", and stop looking at things entirely from your own point of view. Wouldn't our enemies rub their hands with glee if they knew our hate was exhausting us, making us tired and nervous, ruining our looks, giving us heart trouble, and probably shortening our lives? Whilst of course it's difficult to bring yourself to "love your enemy", it's worth at least trying to love yourself. We should never allow the opposition, our enemy if you like, to control our happiness, health and looks.

You can hardly put it better than Shakespeare, who wisely said in the first Act of his play Henry VIII (on the subject of revenge): "heat not a furnace for your foe so hot that it does singe yourself". By exhibiting anger and hatred towards others, we are damaging ourselves. Our health will be affected over time by negative thoughts, such as fear, worry, anger, hatred. 2,500 years ago, the classical Greek philosopher Plato, who along with his mentor Socrates and his student Aristotle, laid the foundations for western philosophy, stated something we all know but ignore: it is that the greatest mistake physicians make is that they attempt to cure the body without curing the mind. The mind and body are one, and should be treated together. We happily swallow pills to temporarily stem or stave off a problem that we have created ourselves in our body without addressing the matter holistically, which is the understanding that the mind, body and spirit are closely connected.

It is a pointless exercise to try and "get even" with a supposed enemy. The often-voiced phrase "don't get mad, get even" is not the right way to move forwards. Getting even has its consequences too, in the same way that the actions of your enemy had an effect on you, and so the dislike or hatred between you can never be concluded: it sits there in your mind unresolved, burning away waiting to raise its head again at some subsequent point. Better to simply cross that person off your list. Make them part of your past, release them in your mind. Simply say to yourself that you are facing the issue and "releasing" them from your life. Step around them until you can be entirely free from their presence, but once you release their "hold" or "influence" over the way you think, you are nearly there. The disappearance of that person from your life will be just a matter of short time.

It is amazing how your business fortunes will change once you take this step, because you have changed the way you think. Your thoughts have become positive, not negative.

- **Hubris**

"Hubris" is a description often given to business leaders who become so arrogant, so consumed by their sense of importance and brilliance, that they cease to look around them, to listen, and become blinded to realities and common sense. Hubris is arrogance, a lack of care or interest in others, and often ends in a spectacular fall from grace. At the height of the great ancient Greek civilization, it was a serious crime punishable under the law to be found guilty of hubris in your dealings where you cause damage to others. This was an advanced civilization with great knowledge and understanding, the wisdom of which appears to be much less understood and appreciated in our modern society. A recent example of hubris that needs little introduction is the downfall of the CEO of the Royal Bank of Scotland (RBS), Sir Fred Goodwin, which has been heavily covered in the media. The impact of his personality had a major effect on the fortunes of RBS, which had been one of the world's leading banks, with consequences which affected many people's lives. It impacted on his own life, and the life of his family too, as his ego and lack of interest in the consequences of his actions on those around him ultimately "rebounded" on him directly. Negative human traits rarely go on for long periods of time without affecting both the fortunes of those around you or yourself. This will be addressed further in the next chapter.

- **Greed and Selfishness**

"Greed" has been defined as a selfish and excessive desire for more of something (such as money) than is needed. As Mahatma Gandhi said, "Earth provides enough to satisfy every man's need but not every man's greed". There are many shocking examples of greed in the modern corporate world, but the story of Kenneth Lay is rarely bettered. Although Kenneth Lay, the convicted former CEO of Enron Corporation died before he served a day in prison for fraud and conspiracy, he will forever be held up to the world as one of the greatest examples of modern unbridled corporate greed.

Greed at the highest levels of industry is often accompanied by a complete lack of awareness of the reality of what that individual is really doing, the effect on others, and how it is viewed by those around that individual. It is as if the individual's unbridled greed was "exempt" from any consideration of wrong doing. This absolute lack of awareness is the starting point in the downward spiral of excessive greed, as the perpetrator has no concept of wrongdoing, and no consideration for anyone except himself. For instance, until the day he died, Kenneth Lay professed to be pure and have done nothing wrong.

Wealth in itself cannot be criticized, even the reported extraordinary material excesses of Kenneth Lay during his time as CEO of Enron, unless it impacts others. It is of course well known how the actions of Lay did in fact impact others however. His comment on his extravagance at his trial was met with a simple explanation: "it was difficult to turn off that sort of lifestyle". The devastation left around him though was a disaster for the corporation and the lives of many employees and others affected by the downturn in the fortunes of Enron Corporation.

The problem is that for all the excess that receives unfavorable comment, there is a powerful alternative message which is portrayed in the media, that greed, when harnessed and regulated, is in fact good for corporations, and even society as a whole. Many commentators defended the huge bonuses paid to employees of banks, even as the 2008/9 financial crisis was in full flow, as part of the necessary performance incentives required to make the financial system work. Books such as Tom Wolfe's "Bonfire of the Vanities" and Michael Lewis's "Liar's Poker", and films like "Wall Street" went further and made greed appear acceptable, almost like a game, perhaps even glorified it, and the lifestyle it brought. And even when performance incentives have not been justified, examples of rewarding of failure are readily available, even in respect of projects being funded by taxpayers, and often remain free from media criticism for reasons not immediately apparent to the public.

However, greed represents a risk to business, and when uncontrolled by decision makers, is likely to contribute to the downfall of a corporation – significant numbers of major banks have in recent times put themselves at risk, or failed, through business decisions related to excessive reckless profit seeking. Some banks have been deemed by western governments as too big to fail, and during the time when the risk taking by individuals at such banks was successful, they received large salaries and bonuses. However, when the risk taking became unsuccessful, and unsustainable, the risk ended up being borne by the government, or rather its tax payers, without any fundamental consequential suffering by the bank's risk takers, who suffered no "claw back" of earnings.

A classic example was the failure of the Northern Rock bank which was taken into British State ownership in February 2008. In this case, a clearly unsustainable long term business model was used to allow excessive short term return, causing the inevitable eventual collapse of the bank when credit sources dried up. The bank's business depended on borrowing money short-term in the interbank market and lending it long-term as mortgage finance. This was an extremely risky strategy as it depended on having access to the wholesale market. Business strategies must always factor in the risk and consequences associated with a critical or fundamental aspect of their business model ceasing to exist or function. Unfortunately, Northern Rock's business strategy/model collapsed when interbank lending effectively ceased as the subprime mortgage market collapsed in the USA and bad debts increased throughout the banking system. Northern Rock was unable to raise sufficient funds to cover its debts as they fell due.

The Northern Rock management's risk strategy was clearly badly flawed and was based on greed – an attempt to make quick profits with little attention to obvious risks. In the six months before the liquidity issues became a problem for the bank, their risky approach had allowed them to gain an unusual nineteen percent of the mortgage market in the UK, even though they were a relatively small second-tier lender. The problem was that the lending policy was flawed and unsustainable, with catastrophic consequences for employees, managers and shareholders. In fact, in the end it may well be that shareholders get nothing for their investment in Northern Rock. On 9th December 2009, nearly two years after the nationalization of the bank, the Financial Times reported that the UK Government's independent valuer of the shares held in Northern Rock were valueless, and shareholders should not be entitled to any compensation for their investments being wiped out when the bank was nationalized. The compensation battle of shareholders will no doubt continue, but the loss of shareholder value can be laid at the door of the bank's management at the time the bank went into State ownership.

If the top executives of the Northern Rock bank had mixed common sense risk analysis with their desire for greater-than-normal short term rates of return, the flaw in their model would easily have been identified. But greed had unfocused them.

The good thing is that not everyone is motivated by greed and short term gain at the expense of the longer term consequences. Society would quickly break down if everyone was as greedy as the few who cause corporate collapses. Most people consider some level of wealth accumulation as desirable by the end of our working lives, but such accumulation is approached with natural caution and consideration of the risks involved.

Acknowledging the impact of greed is important. The root causes of greed must be addressed and satisfactorily treated or fixed, as the international monetary system on which we all rely is only being sustained now, since the 2008/09 financial crisis, through the trillions of dollars of government support worldwide. This money was pumped into the system to offset the risk-taking failures by financial institutions caused through their excessive greed: the short term profit-taking with little thought for the long term consequences.

Behavior must change. As an example of unbalanced behavior, unrelated to balanced long term performance, Wall Street paid out $18 billion in year-end bonuses to its New York employees even though at the end of 2008 the US Government had disbursed $243 billion in emergency assistance to the financial sector. As the financial crisis developed during 2008, the US Government continued to take great care not to upset the interests of the financial institutions or probe too deeply into the reasons why the financial system had collapsed in the way it had. By the beginning of July 2009, the Bank of England had announced in a Report that the banks are still at risk despite more than $14 trillion in support from taxpayers in the UK, USA and Europe. Even if the accountability of governments to their tax payers is put to one side, the way we view risk and profit accumulation must change, because the long term health of the financial system is vital to the western market economy, and it cannot be put at risk by greed.

At the end of November 2009, legislation was finally introduced by the ruling Labour Party for consideration by Parliament, the aim being to "transform" the policing of the financial sector and curb the "casino" activities of banks. This planned legislation includes provisions whereby the Financial Services Authority will be able to amend or cancel bankers' contracts which include excessive pay and bonus deals which threaten the stability of the financial system, and provisions to allow the winding down of banks without disrupting the entire financial system and forcing taxpayers to step in and bail out corporate banking failures.

This legislation was felt necessary by the Chancellor of the Exchequer who expressed disappointment that at the end of 2009, as the global economy was finally recovering from the financial crisis of 2008/09, banks and their executives had not changed their attitudes and behavior. Indeed, on 4th December 2009, just as the Royal Bank of Scotland, which received UK Government liquidity support, announced that it planned to award £1.5billion in bonuses to certain employees, the UK's National Audit Office announced that UK Government support for the UK's banks had reached an astounding £850 billion. The balance between risk and reward appears to still need addressing. The planned UK legislation was a popular measure in view of the media onslaught about the activities of "greedy bankers" who helped to accelerate the economic downturn, but time restraints with a looming election restricted what could be passed into legislation. On 8th April 2010, the British Parliament did however finally pass some limited legislation, the Financial Services Act 2010, which conferred on the Financial Services Authority (FSA) a number of new powers and duties, in particular in relation to so-called "short selling" by financial institutions, a power to suspend firms and individuals, and impose fines, and to set out a financial stability strategy. The new Government elected in May 2010 will continue the process of introducing bank regulation, such as tackling "unacceptable" levels of bank bonuses for employees, and giving consideration to breaking up banks into their retail and investment arms to reduce risk. Greed caused the failings, and vastly increased risk, and this now has a high profile as a result of media coverage of the excesses and information dissemination, forcing governments around the world to act to curb banking excesses.

Similarly, in the USA, Congress is on the brink of passing the most comprehensive regulation of the financial industry since America's Great Depression, including the creation of a consumer protection agency designed to prevent lending abuses that triggered the housing collapse and the worst unemployment in almost three decades. The US government concluded that the deepest problems were associated with failures of regulation, which is why strengthening of regulation was their focus in the preventing of any further financial crisis from arising. This includes regulating derivatives which have been a major contributor to the need for the US government to provide trillions of dollars to bailout the banking system, and will be addressed further later in this book. It remains to be seen however whether this legislation, when it becomes law, will curb the excesses of an industry adept at navigating regulation in pursuit of greed and profit. The remarkable change since the financial crisis of 2008/09 is the awareness of the general public of practices centering around unbridled greed by the few, which has the ability to affect the wider public, and this is why governments are addressing this in new legislation.

But greed affects not just the business world: even the world of politics, which should be expected to pass laws and regulations designed to restrain bankers and businesses from the worst excesses of greed and selfishness, has been exposed and brought down by the human failing of greed. Politicians in Britain exploited the financial rules and regulations set by themselves for their own financial conduct when claiming expenses using taxpayer's funds. The British Parliamentary expenses fiasco which came under public scrutiny in May 2009 when the UK's "Daily Telegraph" newspaper published a leaked copy of the expenses claimed by British Members of Parliament. The greed exhibited by certain members of Parliament caused the downfall of those members, and the loss of trust in this institution.

The greed factor was so powerful, and the desire for secrecy to avoid disclosure, that in February 2008 the House of Commons Authorities actually challenged a decision made by the Information Tribunal to release details of the expenses claims of Members of Parliament following a request under the Freedom of Information Act. The English High Court nevertheless ruled in favour of releasing the MP's expenses claims in May 2008. This was not the end of the matter however. In January 2009, a motion was tabled in the House of Commons by the Leader of the House to exempt MP's expenses from being disclosed under any Freedom of Information Act request (after a previous attempt to obtain exemption had failed in May 2007). The motion was ultimately dropped after large scale public opposition to the motion, and the realization by the Government that opposition parties would vote against the motion. This conduct did not show Parliament in a good light, as it lacked the transparency required of public servants paid for by tax payers and exhibited a continuing desire to hide their conduct behind secrecy.

The fallout from the scandal was enormous, humiliating numerous MP's who were found to have abused their position of trust and authority, and leading The Times newspaper to call the scandal "Parliament's darkest day" in May 2009. In the general election of May 2010, the events of a year earlier had not been forgotten by the general public, and the worst offenders from the "expenses scandal" failed to be re-elected, or stood down from Parliament. It is not difficult to look at the conduct of politicians elsewhere in the world to know that certain lawmakers, just like certain businessmen, can let themselves and society down through this basic human failing.

Uncontrolled greed is always ultimately going to lead to loss, failure and downfall. No one respects the greedy and this trait of human nature should not be accommodated or accepted at any level.

Having addressed in this chapter the negative factors of fear, worry, hatred and anger, hubris, and greed that affect risk and performance of a corporation, we now need to look more closely at why the actions of businessmen can cause a corporation to fail.

CHAPTER 3

HOW PEOPLE CAUSE CORPORATIONS TO FAIL

People are more likely to make or break a corporation by their actions and decisions than external factors. When confronted with failure, managers often blame external factors, such as the operating environment, competition, regulations, changing customer needs and so on. However, whilst these factors may genuinely exist, it is the way that a company responds to adverse external factors which makes the difference between success or failure, rather than the factors themselves. Whether you are operating in the banking sector, construction/services sector, or manufacturing sector, the same key "people" factors arise which cause companies to be unable to deal effectively with difficult trading conditions.

These are:

- Failures of personality;

- Failure of the top executives and management to get the right team in place;

- Failure to understand clearly the business of the company;

- Failure to respond to changed conditions;

FAILURES OF PERSONALITY

A root cause of many corporate failures is the overinflated egos of the top decision making executives and in particular the Chief Executive Officer who runs the corporation. These people may have reached their lofty status through having powerful personalities, and perhaps a commanding presence in front of large groups of people, but that very attribute can also be the cause of their downfall, and that of the corporation they play leading roles in. If any of these people possess an overpowering ego, over the course of time this can put a company at much greater risk of failure if not kept under control.

This is because the bigger their sense of ego, and "invincibility", the less they take note of the opinions and advice of those around them. Arrogance is the belief that "what you don't know isn't important", and leaders who fail are likely to possess this trait in abundance. This leads to:

- Complacency;

- Overriding built-in checks and balances;

- Absence of disagreement;

- Poor communication and the inability to get realistic feedback;

The attitude of the CEO spreads downwards through his direct reports and other senior executives like a cancer. Indeed, it is not unusual for senior executives to attempt to copy the style of the very top executive, such as the CEO, and if this style includes features such as excessive use of fear tactics, arrogance, and the inability to hear alternative view points, it is not long before this style will have detrimental effects on all levels of the workforce.

Complacency:

A major threat to the continued survival of a corporation at any time, even during a time of "plenty" (when leaders should continue to address matters which are seen as obvious and necessary during a period of decline), is the complacency of people inside organizations. The larger a corporation becomes, and the longer any period of profitability lasts, the more senior management tend to believe they cannot fail. People become comfortable. Issues they paid great attention to as the company was growing, such as customer service, quality, and productivity, cease to concern them as much.

Improvement, opportunity for balanced growth, constructive criticism, attention to detail, and change, never stops. Complacency starts at the top, as the leaders congratulate themselves, award undeserved bonuses, start abusing expense allowances, develop the taste for expensive cars, and restaurants and other perks, and become unfocused on things that matter. Things like losing customers. Their attitude tends to be: there's no cause for concern, new customers are coming through the door. But success breeds complacency, and the desire to address continuing change simply becomes too much effort because it appears unnecessary.

If a leader of a company is subconsciously thinking "we're doing just fine", that message is picked up by those around him. His actions will give the game away by how he is using his time. Is he wasting his time on expensive lunches or questionable travel or is he focused still?

Successful companies are constantly addressing ways to stay ahead. Their leaders are focused and not self-congratulatory. They undertake market research and are continually seeking to improve their products and services to meet changing customer needs. They are concerned if a customer doesn't return, is dissatisfied or complains. They listen to staff, motivate them, and ensure their needs are met to keep them happy and productive. The downfall comes when leaders and staff cease to improve, and change, with the changing times. Success leads to people feeling they have found some elusive formula and then progress ceases to happen. At this point in the cycle, failure is just around the corner.

An interesting example is a company that has moved beyond the start-up phase, and has been experiencing growth, increased revenues and profits for a number of years. Staff numbers have been growing. The revenue stream is more secure, and the company is stable. This is the moment of most danger, because the leaders are inclined to "rest on their laurels", and relax. But nothing stays the same. Businesses must continue to evolve, or else they eventually decline and fail. The successes that got a company where it is are in the past, and success is based on your actions today, and in the future. The risk to a company of complacency may be fatal.

Overriding built-in checks and balances:

Checks and balances in a good corporation should include the ability to constructively criticize. However, many organizations avoid vigorous discussion and debate, thereby suppressing ideas and issues which if addressed openly could prevent problems from arising. Raising issues of concern by staff members to top management, or the CEO, can be extremely difficult, because people fear the consequences of criticism, even if done in a constructive manner. Good management should not create fear in staff. It should allow for the ability to express concerns, the ability to listen to what staff have to say, the ability to change direction if appropriate, and the understanding that real dialogue between staff and management can help.

Sometimes checks and balances are put in place primarily to meet legal and regulatory requirement, rather than as a genuine tool to help manage risk faced by the corporation. We can see this from the recent failures in the financial sector. The effectiveness of any risk management program or policy used by a corporation depends on how much the corporation really uses that program or policy in practice. It should not be simply a box-ticking exercise to appease financial services regulators, or auditors, and ensure the "legality" or "constitutionality" of decision making. If the risk management system is not genuinely integrated into business decision making, it won't help prevent losses and problems arising. In the 2008/09 financial sector difficulties, when decisions were taken by executives it appears in some instances that the risk controls were simply overridden, even though in many cases the financial institutions had set up complex governance, risk management and control systems.

The decision makers, often the CEO himself, were too far removed from the input of those providing risk analysis and advice, with the result that decisions were made without a real understanding of risk management by the CEO or the Board of Directors. Or maybe the CEO knew only too well about the risks, but simply ignored the risk advice when crucial decisions were made because he was powerful, and "could" override advice, matters had progressed too far and his ego wouldn't allow the deal to be cancelled, or he was simply "seeking glory". But what is the point of these so-called comprehensive internal checks and balances if they fail to protect you from devastating losses? And why did they fail? Was it just the culture of big bonuses and greed that overrode sensible decision making? Whatever the case, where checks and balances are overridden, sooner or later loss and failure will follow. CEO's and other senior executives are not immune from disaster, and are not "invincible". The importance of checks and balances in a corporation will be addressed further in Part 2 of this book.

Absence of Disagreement:

This follows naturally from the culture of CEO's and other senior management believing they can override built-in checks and balances. Successful executives always have around them people who can advise them on the appropriateness of decisions they are making. These are an inner group who a leader trusts and have the requisite skills base. When crucial decisions are being made, that leader will listen and act accordingly.

An excellent example of "lessons learnt" concerned a well-respected leader, Jack Welsh, who was CEO of General Electric at its peak, who was determined to purchase and integrate the investment bank Kidder Peabody into General Electric, even though the two companies had mismatched cultures. It seems that key members of his trusted inner group of advisers and directors had warned him that the risk involved in this purchase might be inappropriate, but he pressed on with the purchase anyway. The subsequent integration failed, but in recent times he has acknowledged his failure and that hubris had trumped his usual good sense. The decision, although costly, was not fatal to General Electric, but the lesson is that if you have a good team around you, listen to them and heed their advice. Jack Welsh understood this instinctively, and although the built-in checks and balances were overridden in that instance, at least he could not be accused of surrounding himself with people who always agreed with him, and lessons were learnt.

However, weak or ineffective Boards and internal committees can be disastrous. Where the senior executives and inner team surrounding leaders do not voice disagreement, and "rubber stamp" whims and actions of that leader, with no serious discussion of the merits or weaknesses of a proposed action, this is ultimately going to put at risk the profitability and even survival of a corporation, as sooner or later that leader is going to make a mistake.

The failings of the Royal Bank of Scotland (RBS), where the Board failed to adequately question the proposed activities of its CEO, Sir Fred Goodwin, have been well documented. RBS ended 2008 with the biggest loss ever made by a British company (at £28billion), and nobody among his Board or advisers appeared to seriously question his plans. The media fascination with the downfall of Sir Fred Goodwin, and the level of arrogance in his conduct as a CEO, was so great that even a year after his resignation as CEO, he still commanded more news print coverage than any other current CEO in the UK. His self-belief and confidence were allegedly highly infectious, and this powerful personality overrode any doubts in the ranks. The takeover of ABN Amro, which Barclays Bank had pulled out of the bidding for as the price escalated, had a major part to play in the losses incurred by RBS.

It should be the internal advisers who the CEO should be able to rely on to give him rational advice, but this loyal Board of Directors did not appear to be able to put the brakes on a person whom they clearly considered to be a financial genius. They should have been acting as the "counter weight" to the city advisers who, however professional their conduct may have been considered, were earning fees from an acquisition deal so would have had an incentive to see a deal completed. Even so, the lead advisers on this deal have been replaced as RBS's brokers. It is interesting to note that RBS's Chairman at that time was a well known Scottish businessman, but who had little obvious experience in the world of banking at the level required. Bearing in mind that the CEO (as revealed in questioning by the Treasury Select Committee of the House of Commons on 10th February 2009) had no technical bank training and no formal banking qualifications, it would seem prudent to listen to his internal advisers, but this was a group of key executives who showed no inclination to disagree with the CEO's plans. Was it too much to expect that the Board and his close advisers would question the ABN Amro deal at a time when the banking world was already suffering from the collapse of the American housing market (which RBS knew about through the activities of its Citizens subsidiary there) and when losses were already appearing in the accounts of RBS at that time? It may simply be that the deal had progressed so far, perhaps too far for the CEO to pull out, perhaps the CEO just didn't want to pull out, for his own reasons of hubris, even though the evidence pointed to the deal being a major risk to RBS.

Leaving the case of RBS on one side, as a matter of principle, where advice of professionals and the inner team of advisers surrounding key decision makers is spurned, or perhaps worse still the key decision makers do not have effective advisers around them at all, it is merely a question of whether an error of judgment of a key decision maker such as a CEO will be fatal or merely reduce profitability. One thing is for sure, the absence of disagreement is going to cause problems sooner or later. If the CEO cannot listen to, or adequately answer, tough questions, then failure is just around the corner.

Poor communication and the inability to get realistic feedback:

Once again, communication starts at the top. A leader should foster an environment where fear of speaking the truths or realities are not discouraged, where the environment is not a place where people only say what they think the person at the top wants to hear. That way, common sense decisions cannot be made, because no one is basing those decisions on reality. Communication in these instances is based on fear, and fear produces poor decision making. Poor communication is the result of senior management not listening.

Similarly, open and consistent communication to staff is important. If senior management communicate effectively downwards to staff, including the provision of bad news as well as good news, staff are more involved and motivated, and communicate upwardly more effectively about workplace problems and solutions.

When managers pass tasks down the chain of command and then are dissatisfied with the outcome, they should consider whether they communicated the requirements of the task clearly enough before they allocate blame to someone else. It is always possible that *they* did not communicate effectively and left the other person to guess half the story – and were unavailable, unapproachable or had created fear to the extent that the subordinate felt unable to seek clarification.

Employees appreciate an open style of management. Very little information is so confidential that it cannot be disclosed or communicated at all to others, perhaps only information which contains sensitive financial data which may have an effect on share pricing. Apart from disclosures of this sort (which would be both unwise and possibly unlawful), failure to communicate information to other employees is most often a case of management retaining information in the mistaken belief that "information is power".

Internal communication between departments and different divisions within a Group concerning matters such as the transfer of know-how about best management practices, techniques, systems, technical and human resources should be "a given" to help produce growth and profitability. What the failure to disseminate information really does is foster a lack of respect, lack of motivation, a lack of trust and the breakdown of communication avenues that might be more helpful to the senior executive than his ego will allow him to understand.

FAILURE TO GET THE RIGHT TEAM IN PLACE

A further major reason for corporate failures, even where the company is well branded, and appears to have good business and sales strategies, is the existing skill and know-how base of the company's key employees. Success comes from decision-makers surrounding themselves with the right team so they can receive the right advice. The inability of a company to make key senior appointments (or remove identified poor performers in a timely manner) will sooner or later cause failure.

A company must continue to grow, and this means constantly assessing the skills base of key employees already working for the company. To grow, those responsible for the direction of a company will need to deal with changing circumstances, and address new competitive pressures. This may involve entering into new ventures, ventures in conjunction with other companies, and even mergers and acquisitions in order to stay ahead and allow the company to develop.

It is unlikely that, as a company grows and changes with the changing times, the existing employees will have the skills required in-house to cope with change. New blood, new know-how, people with different experiences and flexible mind-sets are required. In making hiring decisions, the easy route of "promoting from within" should be approached with caution. How often do you hear stories of people "being promoted beyond their capability"? Further, an appropriate appointment will not necessarily be achieved by hiring from the "old boy's network", that group of people who are friends and perhaps know each other from school days, city clubs, or restricted membership societies. Coping with change and development requires transparency and the genuine selection of the "right person" for the role required.

A company's leadership should acknowledge lack of know-how or experience and not allow pride or vanity relating to new ("better"?) people to restrict suitable appointments. Pride, vanity, or fear can restrict a company's opportunities to succeed because the leader(s) don't wish to admit they don't know, and can't do, everything. This is also called "arrogance".

FAILURE TO UNDERSTAND CLEARLY THE BUSINESS OF THE CORPORATION

Sometimes appointments are made at the highest levels of corporations that are simply mistakes. The appointee had a good track record elsewhere, but was not suited to the new position he has taken up.

This turned out to be the case with the appointment of Andrew Hornby as CEO of Halifax Bank of Scotland (HBOS). Although he had arrived at HBOS following a successful career at Asda, the supermarket chain, he had no banking qualifications and whilst he had some retail experience within the world of banking, the appointment at the level of Chief Executive Officer within a major banking institution has now been acknowledged as inappropriate bearing in mind his lack of experience for the position and skill base required.

 The problem is that when you don't know the business of the company, or the position to which you have been appointed within the company, well enough, decisions can be made without sufficient knowledge, or are avoided while you learn the new business requirements. At a time when a financial crisis was brewing, and care over lending money was required (HBOS was Britain's biggest mortgage lender at the time), the required leadership was lacking. The CEO, Andrew Hornby, whose skills were undoubtedly correctly described as a marketing expert, ended up taking on a job for which his skills were clearly unsuited in retrospect. The consequent losses (£10.8 billion at the end of 2008) devastated the company, caused its takeover by a competitor, and also left investors in the bank with huge losses. However, whilst the failure of this appointment is plain to see, the error and failings can be traced to his appointment, and perhaps some of the failings should therefore be attributed to those who appointed him, rather than heaping all the blame on this one individual and not acknowledging the errors or lack of hiring discipline of others.

It is interesting to note that since the Financial Services Authority (FSA) in the UK in October 2008 adopted measures which allowed more forthright probing and vetting of senior staff who had applied for "significant influence functions" such as chairmen and chief executives, significant numbers of aspiring senior executives dropped their applications after initial interviews in which they were questioned by the FSA on whether they had the "necessary skills, experience and integrity" for the role applied for. The FSA even went on record in 2009 to say that "In a number of cases, applications for senior roles have been withdrawn following interviews that raised questions concerning the candidate's competence". At last we are at least starting to see a formal process whereby it is being acknowledged, as stated by the FSA, that "it is essential that firms have competent boards". The Financial Services Act of 2010 has now taken the FSA's role further with a wider ability to suspend and fine individuals who are in positions of significant influence.

Where appointed leaders (at all levels within companies) do not adequately understand the business of the company, any number of difficulties can manifest: acting too fast before requisite knowledge is gained; acting too slowly and ending up caught up in the existing status quo and "old guard" attitude within the company; failing to bring in new executives and forming a new team soon enough; or bringing in a new team too soon and misreading the existing company culture and style.

But in the end, poor hiring decisions, where a gamble is taken with the lack of knowledge of the appointee, is an inadvisable course of action.

It may however be that the individual just thought he was smarter than he really was. It may not be just about a lack of common sense such as where bankers committed to credit sources that were not in fact guaranteed to be available. It may be that the complex trading instruments utilized at the time of the financial collapse were simply too difficult to work with, and arrogant traders around the world were playing a high-stakes game they didn't understand.

FAILURE TO RESPOND TO CHANGED CONDITIONS

The one certainty in life is that nothing stays the same. Everything changes. Constantly. You change, nature changes, fashion and tastes change. So being aware of change, expecting and anticipating change, is critical. Change is known to be a major cause of company failure, and the ability to manage change cannot be underestimated.

It could be any number of factors which unsettle existing established routines. Sudden increases in volumes of work, decisions to enter new geographical markets, offering new products or services, working with new clients or new owners of the company, or just working with new managers or a new management team.

Risk varies with each circumstance that changes. Analysis of how to manage these risks will be dealt with in Part 2, but how people react to, and handle the risk of change is equally as important as the formulas for management and control of those risks.

Some people accept change willingly and have a flexible mind set. However, some find change difficult to understand, and remain unwilling to change, and immoveable. The unwilling will test management's resolve, and how management deal with this risk will dictate the success of the transition. Negative and destructive employees must be coached and counseled into accepting change, and quickly moved through the stages of denial, anger, desire for compromise, and fear to the point of final acceptance. Where this proves not possible, the employee must be moved quickly to the exit door.

When a new leader arrives, whether at the level of CEO or divisional level or departmental level in your organization, there is little point in strongly resisting change, as that new person is not going to leave in such a short time that you can take the view that you will "ride out the storm". New leaders often make decisions quickly as to who they want as part of their team and who is to be discarded, even when they have vowed to take their time. Early impressions will therefore count, and your past record of achievement will be of minimal significance. The new boss will want to hear that you are "on board" and prepared to be part of his team and support him. He won't want to hear about past problems you have encountered, mistreatment, poor pay and so on. He will simply want you to accept the changed circumstances and support him. Any signs of waiver in your support, or giving an impression that you are invaluable and untouchable, will be received badly and may be fatal. Leave your ego at the door.

Changed faces at the top of your management mean changed circumstances. You must decide whether your new boss's style, vision, and business practices are ones you want to live with, and then commit to supporting his plans or leave. It's as simple as that. You have to put the past behind you, and accept the present situation. Attempting to ride out the storm with a negative attitude will cause everyone immense difficulties, and you will end up being moved along anyway. But if you decide to stay, become part of the new team and take a positive approach to the changed circumstances, it is worth remembering that humans are very adaptable as soon as you firmly put the past behind you.

Even where change comes about from a changed business strategy, perhaps even from a leader "seeking glory", such as through a merger or acquisition in which not everyone is in agreement with the strategy, discipline of management must always be maintained. Business must continue to be conducted professionally. New deals must be rigorously analysed, and flawed projects rejected.

Management must also recognize when change isn't working, be prepared to take hard decisions to curtail the direction they are going in, and be flexible enough to consider alternative approaches and strategies.

***

The last two chapters have discussed human failings which cause failure. The discussion must now be moved in a more positive direction. The next chapter discusses how the use of positive human attributes can materially assist a company's success.

CHAPTER 4

POSITIVE HUMAN TRAITS: REDUCING RISK THROUGH YOUR CONDUCT

In the same way that negative human traits can cause corporate failure, positive human traits can bring personal and corporate success.

The keys to greater personal and corporate success are straightforward and readily attainable. They do however require you to pay attention in the way you conduct your life. The risk of inappropriate action which causes loss, failure, and chaotic, unproductive or unhappy working environments can be significantly reduced by following the suggestions outlined below, which are important matters to understand in reducing "people risk" to organizations.

The keys are as follows:

- Learn about yourself;

- Develop an awareness of others;

- Develop the right attitude;

- Learn about your "image";

- Learn simplicity;

LEARN ABOUT YOURSELF

To achieve real success, you must first look inwards and get to know yourself. Finding out about yourself reduces the risk in business dealings. As will be seen in the next section which focuses on developing an awareness of others, what you give out is what you are going to get back, so getting to know yourself is vital. Unless you know who "you" really are, how can you give of your best? How can you find the right environment to "shine" in? Those you work with, those around you, should never "know" or "see" you in a different light than how you know or see yourself. You must be realistic about who you are, and be honest about faults as well as attributes. People usually know more about you than you would care to realize.

Getting to know who you really are is vital to living a balanced, happy life, and only when you discover the true "you" can you get on the right path which leads to fulfillment and, hopefully, happiness. Happy people are good to work with, and that can only benefit an organization.

Whilst material goals and career success are natural goals, they should not be your only goals. Life must have a balance. We tend to rely on material rewards, climbing the corporate ladder, and the approval of others in what we are doing, to judge our level of "success" in life. But if we looked inwards a little more often, rather than outwards all the time, we would discover that life can be much more fulfilling when we trust our own judgment, rely on our own instincts, and make independent decisions rather than depending on opinions or approval which are gone almost as soon as they arrived.

Success doesn't depend on the size of your income, house or car, but once you start to understand your own strengths and abilities, happiness (and material success if that is important to you) will surely follow.

Your true self is always there, waiting to reveal itself to others, and indeed is often actually revealing itself to others, whether you like it or not. So it is worth getting to know who you really are, because others are going to see that person anyway sooner or later. Your path forwards in an organization is not easy to alter once you have revealed your true self to others, or the real "you" becomes apparent. Time is too valuable to waste while the years roll by in fruitless endeavor, so start understanding Who You Are now.

As an aside from the main focus of this section, the true "you" should be matched to your talents, and if you are not on the right path, neither you nor the organization you work for are truly benefitting. If you should conclude that your best path is in another direction, have faith in yourself to move on and reach your potential, so that when you reach your retirement years you don't feel you have wasted too much time.

But back to the focus of this section, which is learning about yourself: What normally happens in the business world, in organizations or corporations, is that people adopt a "persona", or perhaps several "personae", depending on whom they are dealing with. People may well act one way with their subordinates, another way with those above them in the organization, another way with their immediate boss, and perhaps a totally different way with people outside their organization.

The true "self", of both you and others, is certainly going to reveal itself at some point, in some way or another, and you are going to come face to face with that real person (either you or someone else) and have to deal with it. You need to be awake and listening at this time. If it is "you" that is being "revealed", make sure you understand what was revealed and whether you are therefore on the right path. There is always time to change if what you discover suggests that another path is better.

But if someone is revealing something about *their* true self to *you*, this is what you really want to see or hear, because you want to know what someone really means when they say something, which may well be different from the words that came out of their mouth.

Whatever the context of your business dealings, whether you are negotiating a contract, at a job interview, buying or selling, or just doing what someone is telling you to do, you want to understand what their character and motivation is: where they are "coming from" – you want to know the other person's real self.

Once you discover the real self of the person with whom you are dealing, the risk involved in doing business is greatly reduced, because you can put the way they act, what they say, into the correct context. And vice-versa. Once others understand the true "you", doing business with you becomes much less of a risk for them, so you should make an effort to learn about who you really are, because as mentioned earlier, sooner or later you are going to reveal that "person" to others, either inadvertently or openly.

Observation. It is worth being observant. Every situation you find yourself in has the potential to reveal something about you and about others. Observance is very relevant to awareness, and will be explained further below in the discussion on "awareness", but it should be noted now that it doesn't take much to allow you to see beneath the surface and discover useful information about someone else. It could be what someone is unconsciously saying, or doing, the way someone reacts to a question or comment, the way they act in the "down time" in a meeting when everyone relaxes a bit.

Pointers to obtaining insight into others abound at all times, and can be used by anyone who tunes into them. Make sure that the person who uses these insights is *you*, whether or not others have picked up any insights. If others *have* picked up any insights, this is not a matter for concern unless you are unaware of the signals you are revealing. You will not know this unless you have taken time to learn about yourself, to learn who the true "you" is that you are subconsciously revealing to others. Knowing the real you reduces your risk of failure.

So who really are you? Do you act differently at home than when you are at work? If so, why? Are you worried you might reveal your true self to someone at work? Acting differently in this way is not a good way to conduct yourself, because many people spend a large portion of their lives at work, and trying to hide who you really are for large parts of every day will not create peace of mind or happiness.

You are going to produce a better work product when you are happy, so eliminate from your daily life actions you take which you are not instinctively comfortable with.

Approval. The most obvious and important thing to remember, which affects many things people do both consciously and unconsciously, is that you do not need to be approved or affirmed by people to be happy.

Whilst "approval" or "affirmation" by others of what you do can clearly make you feel good, it can lead you into a trap whereby everything you do is designed with the goal of seeking approval from someone: your boss, your subordinates, your "friends".

Unfortunately this is your "ego" ruling you, and it is not the real you. You find the real "you" only when you take the time to strip away unnecessary aspects of your ego. You don't have to be the most popular person in town to be happy. By releasing your ego, you cannot be manipulated or controlled, you do not seek approval as a means to being "happy". This "release" involves (1) letting go of control of others, (2) letting go of the need for approval, and (3) letting go of the need to be judged. You need to be aware of these features of your personality, and to block, neutralize or eliminate them every time they arise. Failure to do so will have a material impact on your life.

If you are happy within yourself, it is far more difficult for your life to be controlled by others, and you will be less affected by the vagaries of life, the ups and downs. Things are going to go wrong from time to time, and being happy with yourself, the person you really are, will allow you to overcome a reversal in your fortunes.

The sooner you learn about who you really are, the sooner you can reduce the risk of making mistakes you aren't aware you are making, the risk of going down paths that are inappropriate for you; and both you and your organization will be the beneficiaries.

DEVELOP AN AWARENESS OF OTHERS

One of the biggest obstacles facing us is the ability to interact with others. What you give out is ultimately what you are going to get back. How much attention do you pay to those around you? How much are you aware of those around you? Do you know when someone is unaware of you?

Awareness about others is very important. To create a good, productive, working environment, we must interact effectively with people we come into contact with.

A surprising number of executives do not have any noticeable sense of awareness. They lack awareness of what is really going on around them. Either they are too busy talking ("listening to themselves") to listen to anyone else, or too involved in their own corporate "persona" or presence to notice what someone else might be doing.

These executives increase risk to their companies by their lack of awareness, because "people" are what business is about, and you can't be effective in business without understanding what is going on around you.

Lots of information is readily available to you by being aware of what people are saying, doing, or not saying or not doing. The best results come from knowing the people you are working with better, whether you are negotiating with them, managing them, directing their activities, or simply working together with them.

Listening. Awareness is developed by listening. The ability to listen, to the point where you actually hear and understand what someone is saying, is one of businesses most vital requirements. It is so vital, and so obvious, that it can be said without any serious debate that people doing business deals will achieve different results if the executive is listening as opposed to an executive that is not. So important is this ability that many top executives will list it as a primary reason for their success, confirming the oft repeated mantras such as "good things happen when you pay attention"; "the best salespeople are great listeners – that's how you find out what a buyer wants"; and "learn to become a good listener".

Yet still many executives are so pleased with themselves, so intent on feeding their already inflated ego and arrogance, that they have forgotten this vital attribute. They happily talk about themselves, rarely wait until the other person has finished talking, have no embarrassment at interrupting someone in the middle of a sentence. They rarely make the other person feel important, they are far too busy trying to be important themselves. They use the words "I", "me", and "myself" far too readily. These people are rarely liked, and are a risk to a company's business.

What such people do not fully appreciate is that other people can pick up when someone is not tuned in, not listening fully. And if anyone thinks that people don't notice your true character, you would be sadly mistaken – just listen to what people say in the corridors, by the coffee machine, privately – then you would be shocked to know how much people "know" about your true character, and things you do that you thought they were unaware of. Whilst gossip is not desirable in an organization, it happens, and the way people discuss you in the corridors will vary depending on your attitude. Developing awareness is about many things, but listening is a fundamental aspect of becoming aware. Listening, really listening to what people are saying, reduces risk and increases the likelihood of success.

Nobody is perfect, and there are things we have all done in the past which we would perhaps prefer hadn't happened, or weren't revealed. When these matters are revealed however, we must be honest, accept the truth, and allow people's thoughts to move on. Denial ensures that your progress in both your company and life is restricted.

A recent expression being used in industry training of managers is called "mindfulness training". The perceived benefit of mindfulness training in the work environment is the ability to become more conscious of a person's communication with others so that they are responding with awareness rather than simply reacting, and through better communication you create the knock-on effect of less conflict and stress in the work environment, and this in turn leads to better teamwork, productivity and leadership.

These benefits are astounding for a business, but they do require that senior executives limit the impact of their ego, arrogance, greed and selfishness, become more honest and transparent, and actually take note of what is going on around them instead of solely focusing on their own wants and needs.

Mindfulness can be summed up *as the ability to listen, to watch, to wait and to learn.*

Observing. We have talked about the impact of listening. Greater power in negotiations is also derived from "observing". Noticing, without judgment, the experiences and feelings that pass through your mind and body. Observing means seeing a bigger picture, taking the experiences and feelings, conscious and unconscious signals you receive, and converting them into something usable.

The power of observation in developing awareness should not be underestimated. Sometimes it is important to travel, great distances if necessary, to actually physically observe someone face to face that you are doing business with, even when you could have satisfactorily done the business over the phone. This physical meeting is important because your view of the people with whom you are doing business is likely to alter, the impressions you form will be different, as a result of what you observe even more than what you hear.

Observing and listening are therefore two vital functions in reducing risk in business. Much can be gained from what you learn as a result of meeting someone in person.

But there is no point in meeting someone if you do not develop your powers of observation. People are constantly revealing themselves in ways that will go unnoticed unless you are fully tuned into noticing things they are revealing, consciously and subconsciously. The subconscious, or unconscious, signals that people give off are often called people's "body language". There are many books available on this subject.

The conscious signals are even easier to pick up – things that people do intentionally – but most executives miss these signals because they have not developed the power to listen and observe. For instance, how someone is dressed, how they greet you or shake your hand, what kind of a presence they command, how they stand and sit, the pace and confidence of their speech, whether their demeanor is happy, aggressive, nervous, timid, casual or too eager will reveal information to you. All these signals tell you something if you take the time to notice, to register this information in your mind. It has the potential to change your deal depending on whether or not you are listening and observing.

Keep aware at all times when meeting people. There will be further discussion about negotiation techniques to reduce risk in the next chapter, but observing the way people operate, conduct themselves, talk, dress and even relax can be very revealing and is likely to assist you. As mentioned earlier, there are always periods of down time during meetings when no business is being conducted. Observe how people you are doing business with conduct themselves at this time – are they happy, annoyed, sharp with their colleagues? Is this going to make things easier or more difficult?

Never forget the signals you get from other people's eyes, as eyes tell you a lot about what people are thinking, even when what they are saying gives little away. When you are meeting people from another organization, rather than your own organization, the observation of how they address each other, and how they look at each other, will tell you how much progress you are making (or lack of it). It is hard to hide what the eyes reveal.

Not every deal comes together immediately, and occasionally executives must take a longer term approach. Sometimes this requires a leader to focus on broader goals than short term profit maximization, seeing beyond what is mathematically measurable in monetary terms, and looking at the human equation.

Business leaders always need to look at the wider picture, to see beyond the immediate results to the longer term consequences of their decisions. They need to understand how to integrate mindfulness features into their decision making to achieve results which provide human benefit as well as monetary benefits. Executives may not be around forever, particularly if they always think "short term", but corporations hope to be around after their current employees have gone, and developing mindfulness assists longer term goals.

Patience. Finally, the other important component of developing awareness, in addition to listening and observing, is learning patience, the ability to "wait". Learning the ability to resist the urge to react or act in haste. Patience is often required when interacting with people.

A really good negotiator or manager of people will become aware of internal thoughts and feelings, both positive and negative, and rather than reacting immediately to those thoughts and feelings, he will wait and consider the wisest option for action as a result of his thoughts and feelings. How the picture he has developed from the input he has received can best be utilized. This will enable him to discover the best way to deal with the person he is doing business with, make him feel comfortable, and achieve the best results, based on what he sees and hears.

Patience and calmness in your actions and decision making is vital, and reacting quickly brings with it the risk of business failure. The pressure on managers to make a quick decision, any decision, is often immense. This pressure must be resisted, and haste avoided. Big decisions must be made logically and analytically. This requires patience. Quick, "decisive", actions or decisions by businessmen are often considered necessary, but someone who feels they need to make quick decisions should examine why this is necessary. Is it because they are afraid of what others are thinking, too insecure to allow themselves the time to sensibly assess a situation? Hasty decisions (which unaware managers might call "decisive" decisions) may often lead a company to have to live with the bad decision and the consequences for a long time. "Undoing" the damage caused by hasty decision-making takes a long time, and can be a painful process for a company.

From time to time we cross paths with particularly difficult people who you do not "resonate" with. This is where your powers of patience become beneficial. Indeed, how you react to the presence of such people around you may define the future you have within an organization. Many people are unaware of the true self within them, and are living their life based on conditioning, beliefs and values instilled in them from an early age. They may not have ever stopped to think about whether those beliefs and values actually help them, or are suitable for their personality and talents. Their conditioning, their upbringing, may have created characteristics which are unbalancing their real inner self, and which makes them undesirable people to be in the presence of. This is because they lack awareness of those around them, have negative human traits that have been previously discussed, and are probably following habits and styles they picked up unconsciously as they grew up.

So patience is particularly required when interacting with these persons. The easiest way to deal with someone like this is to ignore them, step around them, and as far as possible cut them out of your life, because their presence is not going to add to your sense of well being. However, if you can't avoid them, because for instance they are a close work colleague, and there is no way to interrupt or change their patterns of speech and behavior, then just observe them dispassionately, be patient and do not become annoyed. Anger directed internally is not healthy, and anger directed externally will have untold consequences, so neither form of anger is helpful. You simply have to remember to be "yourself" at all times, never lose touch with your own inner qualities, and the problem will dissipate in time. Remember, nothing ever stays the same for very long.

In conclusion on the subject of awareness: developing

awareness, becoming mindful of others, assists business success and reduces risk of failure because you gather a wider "picture", a greater knowledge of what is going on around you.

This involves learning **to listen, to watch, and to wait**. Then true learning, true knowledge, will come, and with it success.

DEVELOP THE RIGHT ATTITUDE

A positive attitude is far more likely to result in a positive outcome, regardless of how difficult the hurdles may be, and a negative attitude is likely to result in a negative outcome, even when there appears to be nothing to hinder you.

So what is a positive attitude and what is a negative attitude? We instinctively know what is the right attitude, because as mentioned above in the section on awareness, people in organizations react differently to different people, resonate differently with different people, and are quicker to criticize someone (in the corridors, around the coffee machines, behind closed doors, in cafes and bars after work and so on where people gossip) who has a negative attitude as opposed to someone who has a positive attitude or approach to working with others. And they are just as likely to say positive and encouraging things behind your back, rather than criticism, if you have a positive attitude. Gossip is not a good attribute in a person, but when people gossip it can be a useful indicator of whether you come into the "positive" or "negative" category in people's minds.

The bottom line is that positive people attract success and negative people attract failure. The risk to an organization increases with every negative person it employs – even one negative personality in a key position may push a company from success to failure. People should be employed to increase the prospect of success and reduce the risk of failure, but some people's attitude does exactly the opposite – it increases the prospect of loss and failure, and creates working environments that are chaotic, unproductive and unhappy. And still the organization pays them to work there!

Your approach to the following issues will define whether you are "positive" or "negative" person.

- Failure

- Competition

- Appreciation

- Approval

- Attention

- Control

- Worry

- Change

- Blame

Failure: Mistakes happen, but can you acknowledge a mistake and learn from the failure? Can you say you were wrong, that you need help or that you don't know something? Openness and transparency are important, and not being able to admit you don't know something can lead to suspicion about what you actually do know. Most people will accept that someone has made a mistake, but it is how you deal with the mistake that will be noticed. So don't try and blame others, or rationalize the mistake, or, worse still, cover it up until a minor problem causes major damage. Acknowledge, learn, and move on.

Competition: Do you always have to be right? Do you disagree or react badly to criticism? Do you disagree because it wasn't your idea? Are you rigid, inflexible, take things too personally? Do you see colleagues as "rivals" who must be defeated? Do you belittle others, or criticize? Are you judgmental of others or manipulative? Do your actions tend to reduce the self esteem of others? Do you try and "point score" from working a "macho hours culture"? Persistent long hours means your life is out of balance.

Appreciation: Do you praise people in their absence as well as in their presence? Do you pass on compliments received from senior management? Does what you say enhance the self esteem of others and make them feel accepted, competent, worthwhile and appreciated? Do you recognize the achievements of others?

Approval: Are you constantly seeking or "fishing" for compliments rather than acting with humility? Are you looking for approval? Do you talk too much so as to attract other people's attention rather than being silent when you have nothing relevant to say? Do you praise yourself?

Attention: Must you always be the centre of attention? Do you try and impress with your smart car, house or looks? Can you sit quietly and listen? Can you share the limelight with others?

Control: Do you need to control others or do you give them freedom to think independently? Do you have to know what others are doing every moment or do you trust them to act sensibly? Can you delegate difficult or critical tasks?

Worry: Do you worry over trivialities? Do you have mood swings, or moan about your lot? Do you constantly feel hurried, driven to do things? Do you feel under pressure from your superiors? Learn to relax.

Change: Do you cling to the past or do you acknowledge that change happens, that nothing stays the same forever? Are you flexible? Do you procrastinate on simple or important tasks, decisions or initiatives?

Blame: Do you blame others rather than accept responsibility for your own circumstances and actions? Do you think when something goes wrong that you are the victim of circumstance, or bad luck? The sooner you accept responsibility for what happens in your life, rather than blaming others, the sooner that success will come your way.

From the above scenarios, you can easily conclude whether you would be considered a positive or negative person by work colleagues.

Two important final points in relation to "attitude":

Firstly, the golden rule to follow is *only do to other people those things that you would be happy to see done to you.*

Secondly, *smile.* Someone who smiles a lot tends to have a more positive effect on others than a person who is always serious. There is nothing wrong with smiling, it makes everyone's day better and gives those around you the impression that you have a positive attitude – which smiling will ensure you do have!

LEARN ABOUT YOUR IMAGE

When did you last really look at yourself? When did you last really assess what image you are portraying to those around you? If you don't care for yourself and respect yourself, why should others?

Are you giving the right impression or "lead" for your subordinates to follow? It is a good idea to think of yourself as a "brand" that must be carefully managed, so that others want to follow you, aspire to what you represent, "buy into" your image, vision and direction on the basis of what they see in front of them. Treat yourself the way you would like to see your company's products treated.

Does your image portray fitness and discipline or unfitness, sloth and lethargy? You need to find the balance between home life and work life, and if you have been neglecting your relaxation time, and failing to look after your mind and body, it is likely you are not performing at your best. Are you showing signs of fatigue? Fatigue lowers physical resistance to illness and resistance to worry, undesirable emotions and fear. Additionally, it does not benefit your image and appearance.

The tipping point between health and fitness and overwork and under performance is very tight – your value to a company can easily be eroded as your image changes from the healthy, fit specimen you once were to something less appealing. And it can never be said too many times that the image you portray affects the image of your company.

So take time to portray yourself in the best light at all times:

- Dress well;

59

- Smile to put those around you at ease;

- Move in a relaxed manner, take your time, rather than rushing around;

- Use your eyes, look at people when you meet them;

- When speaking, speak briefly and don't ramble;

- Keep fit and look healthy – excessive food and alcohol are signs of ill discipline.

These small steps will give you a desirable image and enhance both your continuing prospects of success, and those of your company. Your overall "presence" plays a larger part in the success of your company's business, their success in negotiations around the world, than you might care to believe. People remember appearance more often than your words.

LEARN SIMPLICITY

Everyone should develop good working habits. This reduces the risk of mistakes, miscommunication and disorganization. The most important working habit is to learn clarity and simplicity.

The mind must be uncluttered to be able to make decisions effectively, so keep your office and desk clear of unnecessary clutter. Undertake regular clear outs, and be ruthless about what you no longer need to hold on to. Are those papers, books and files really still useful?

Prioritize. Only retain on your desk those papers that relate to the immediate problem at hand. The "problem at hand" should always be the most important matter that you are facing. Often people postpone the most important task because it will be difficult or time consuming, and they fool themselves that they are being active and useful because they have completed some lesser, easier, tasks during the day. Always prioritize your work according to importance. Don't be afraid to delegate a task if there are pressing deadlines for various tasks and you must focus on a more urgent priority.

Keep your life as simple as possible. We allow ourselves to be constantly distracted by unimportant and meaningless things, rather than using our time wisely on what will really make a difference in our lives. Don't waste your time and energy on things that can't be changed, but concentrate on what you can make a difference with, things that can improve your life. The mind is constantly being diverted from what matters *now*, while we worry about some event in the future which may never arrive. Simplicity means living in the present.

* * *

There is one final thought which is worth recounting. It derives from an old story which has been recounted in many different ways but goes along the following lines: an angel comes to a person just before he dies and asks three questions:

- Is the world a better place because of your life?

- Is the world a better place because of the efforts you exerted?

- Is the world a better place because you were around?

It would be nice to answer positively to all these questions.

CHAPTER 5

HOW TO NEGOTIATE TO REDUCE RISK

Everyone has their own ideas about how to negotiate, and there are already enough books readily available on the subject, so this chapter won't add to that overflowing pile of literature. However, we do need to remind ourselves constantly of the importance of *people* in negotiating business deals. Forget the importance of *people* at your peril as you put together your business strategy. Part 1 of this book is about the impact and risk *people* pose to the success or failure of corporations, and this is nowhere more apparent than in the way people conduct business (or personal) negotiations.

From a personal perspective, after many years of travelling all over the world, to a hundred countries or more where a vast range of different cultures were encountered over three decades, often participating in negotiations which were complex and involved vast sums of money, one thing became increasingly clear as the years passed by: *people* can be the biggest risk to successful negotiating.

People are the dominant factor in whether negotiations are concluded successfully or collapse in failure. People constantly blame external factors for their failures, but a brief examination of their conduct, their own response to situations they face, is likely to reveal the true reason why they were less happy with an outcome than they should have been, or failed completely, or, to put it another way, managed to avoid being successful.

The importance of awareness, attitude and image has been addressed in the previous chapter, but risk in negotiations can be greatly reduced by paying attention to these attributes, in the same way that these attributes are vital to every other area of business and corporate life.

The key to reducing the risk of failure, and therefore increasing the chances of success, is to understand that winning over the people on the other side of the table will go a long way to winning you a good deal.

How is this done? By utilizing the same formula that should apply in every area of your corporate and personal life: *listen, watch, wait and learn.*

Preparation: Negotiations start long before you get into the meeting room. Preparation is essential. Are you too busy to prepare effectively or too tired on arriving at the venue? Failure to prepare because of other more pressing matters or tiredness is an excellent way to ensure you will not perform well and will not return the investment that your employer has made in you.

Many years ago a well respected and well travelled diplomat once said: "The first thing to decide before you walk into any negotiation is what to do if the other fellow says "no"".

Never a truer word was uttered, and if you haven't prepared for all eventualities, then you are increasing the risk that your company will finish up with a deal it is not happy with.

In my years of travel to meetings where negotiations were due to take place, I have frequently been surprised by how many company representatives (the "face" of the company) have not read the papers carefully which form the basis of the negotiations they are there for, and some people hadn't read the papers at all! How could they later complain that the deal they agreed to contained some "small print" they didn't like?

Make sure you know what you are signing up to. The time to concern yourself with the small print of a deal is *before* you put pen to paper, not afterwards when you are blaming some external factor for the problems you are facing, or trying to justify the deal to an irate Board of Directors. If you are not absolutely sure about the terms of what you are signing, get someone else to review the deal you are signing and check you didn't miss some important point, even involve a lawyer to give you his view – it will be much cheaper advice before you sign a contract than afterwards when you are asking for the lawyer's help to extract you from the deal or to settle claims or law suits.

People often think you can do much of the negotiation over a telephone before you meet. Be careful about this tactic, as it invariably causes disappointment or even a breakdown in trust when the terms are finally reduced to writing, as those terms are often different from what you thought was the position you had agreed to.

Arrival: First impressions are very important. You want the other parties to treat you with interest and consideration. So it will not be helpful to portray a negative attitude, with a glum, humorless face. Give the impression of confidence by walking slowly and confidently to the meeting room table, smile warmly, show friendliness and dress well.

There is no need to try and start the business discussions immediately. Get to know the participants in the meeting room, find out about them, ask questions and tell them a little about you, if you are asked. General "chit-chat" can be very valuable sometimes, and allows you the opportunity to observe who you are really dealing with. It also helps to relax you as well as being sociable, and it's a rare person who isn't happy to talk at a social level before getting the real meeting underway. Watch their "body language". How is their demeanor, are they comfortable or anxious, do you think it will be easy to negotiate with them or are they likely to be difficult? Eyes will tell you about how a person is thinking, as people use eyes to communicate even more than words. The ability to look someone in the eye tells them that you are honest, and makes them comfortable. Notice whether they look you in the eye.

Observation at all times is vital. You learn from this. The need to develop "awareness" was discussed in the last chapter, and awareness should reduce your risk if you listen and observe. The more you know, the less the risk of failure, because you are operating from a point of greater knowledge and certainty. Be aware of your internal thoughts and feelings, your senses and instinct as you get to know someone. You can learn almost all you need to know, and probably more than others would like you to know, simply by watching and listening, and by being careful about what you say yourself.

During the Meeting: How easy it will be to do a deal with someone with whom you are negotiating will be indicated by such things as how secure or insecure that person is with their position, whether he knows or doesn't know what he wants to achieve, whether he can take reasonable risks, or is he reluctant to commit even mundane details. These facts will indicate the speed and likelihood of completing the deal.

Certainly not all meetings go as well as you would like, and some go extremely badly. This may be because you do not "resonate" with your counterpart for some reason. It is imperative to continue to give your company the best chance of success by always acting with diplomacy and never provoking the other person. Never allow yourself to blurt out some indiscretion, "say it how it is" – you will regret that. The moment you make a disparaging comment, or become angry, the battle is lost and obtaining a fair deal will take longer. If patience is not an attribute of a negotiator, that person is almost certainly not suitable to be a negotiator. However this doesn't mean that as a negotiator you can't be firm regarding the position you take. You must simply never exhibit anger, aggression or act in a provocative manner. Negotiations are often adversarial, and not everyone is suited to that environment. However, if you have to stand your ground rather than compromise beyond a sensible and fair position from the point of view of your organization, do this in a suitably diplomatic manner so that the impression you leave behind at the end of the discussion is one where the other side feels able to continue to communicate with you at a future time as the sides "grind out" a deal.

Another way to get an impression of how things are going is by observing the "fringe times", such as the breaks in a meeting, interruptions and the start and end of meetings. At these times people may have their guard down more, and they may give you unintended indications of your progress (or lack of it).

Above all, understand the things you can change and the things that you can't. Accept what you can't change.

Time: "Time" is a great pressure on negotiations. If you have a deadline to meet, a plane to catch, be prepared for your negotiation to be unsuccessful. Conclusions to negotiations are rarely reached within the time allotted, so be prepared to be patient. You will put your company's position at risk by trying to "speed up" negotiations – you inevitably end up "giving away" items, and before you realize it, maybe you will even give away the "store" if you lose your discipline.

No one likes to be rushed, so just slow down to the pace that the business is being conducted at and start listening to what the other side are saying rather than fretting over the delay to your next appointment. Was that next appointment (whether personal or business) that important? So important that you are prepared to put at risk the current negotiations? Flexibility and patience are essential.

Another reason why time may be passing without a satisfactory conclusion may be because you are not listening to what is being said. If you *really* listened, read between the lines, you might spot the problem, amend your position or proposal and achieve a satisfactory outcome. This doesn't mean "concede", it means understanding what the other side require to make things work. If you have listened long enough, believe you understand what is required and can't make a decision there and then, simply halt the meeting and go away and think about the solution. It is better to not be rushed into decision-making, and if delay means you lose the deal, then you must let it go. It is also always acceptable to say "no".

Even when you are the dominant party, never treat the other side with disrespect, or unduly pressure them. Offer fair deadlines to accept the deal that is proposed where ever possible. Even if your "pressured" conduct is not unlawful, it's surprising how often the boot is on the other foot sooner than you would think. In any event, no one should allow themselves to develop a reputation for arrogant conduct.

Only "ego" forces you to conclude things quickly when a cooling off period to reconsider the deal might have been more sensible. A lot of deals get done because someone's ego was so bloated that they could not afford psychologically *not* to get the deal done. The Board, senior management, colleagues and so on back in the office expected a deal to happen, and pride therefore necessitated that a deal should happen. Many companies have been the beneficiary by understanding the other negotiator's ego, and taking legitimate advantage of it. A negotiator's armory should always contain the word "no". It is also important to make sure that you are not the one letting ego get in the way either, even if you have spotted the deficiency on the other side.

Often a "man in a hurry" may raise suspicion. Sometimes this causes negotiations to move even slower, or at worst, stop altogether. The other party may start to think that they missed something in the small print of your proposal or your contract, and so decide to refer it to their lawyer or a higher layer of management. It is much better to operate in a relaxed manner. Final approval of the deal you negotiate may require that the deal is looked at and approved by someone who is not present at the meeting anyway. This may even be a specific negotiating strategy to reduce the risk of a hurried decision which can be regretted at leisure.

Finally, don't overstretch a meeting in the hope of concluding a deal "there and then". Stretching out a meeting to the point where everyone is tired will ensure that the irritation between the parties is likely to be present, and could even cause breakdown of negotiations.

Being "mentally fresh" is important, as you have to live with what you negotiate long after the ink is dry on the contract. Tiredness certainly increases risk, as mistakes are more likely to occur, or missing an important point which would not have occurred if you were fresh.

"Goodwill" concessions or "Toughness"?: Are "goodwill" concessions going to be perceived as softness? Is a tough stance going to produce deadlock? This is where "awareness" of whom you are dealing with matters. As stated earlier in this chapter, the sooner you can sense the nature of the negotiator you are dealing with, the better your chance of understanding how proposals you offer to close issues will be perceived. You should always know what issues are essential to your deal beforehand, and what can in fact be "conceded" without risk. If you have prepared well for the negotiation, you will never be increasing your company's risk profile until you concede on an essential element of the deal from your company's perspective. If you have conceded on an issue and then negotiations on subsequent issues still get bogged down even though you had already made a "goodwill concession", you can always "take back" the concession if it seems the appropriate thing to do: sometimes it can bring the other side "back to reality". It's all part of the tricky dynamic of extracting a satisfactory deal for your organization.

Negotiating Overseas: The pressures associated with travelling and negotiating deals are obviously vastly different from the pressures of sitting in an office in your home town. This is so obvious that it has always surprised me when executives in the home office make unrealistic negotiating demands on travelling negotiators, often after the negotiator has already left the home office and arrived at the overseas venue, and the negotiations are about to commence. If the home office executives put themselves in the traveler's position, it would not take them long to realize that not only are their commercial or contractual demands impossible to sell to the hosts, but may even put the whole negotiations in jeopardy. In order to understand what can and can't realistically be achieved in an overseas environment, there is no better way than to see for yourself. You don't really understand how people in other parts of the globe think and work until you've been in their environment, talked to them and learned from them. You can learn wherever you go overseas, from local people that cross your path, to cab drivers, shop keepers and of course the people who you are trying to do business with.

Plan well before you travel. Travel light, drink lots of water, and however hard it may appear, adjust your mind to the new time zone immediately on arrival. If you have a negative approach to travel, and are worried about how you will cope, your experience is likely to mirror the way you are thinking. Approach every business trip with a positive attitude, an opportunity to learn. Life is not just about making money, it is also about learning, about extending the boundaries of your understanding of different cultures and environments, and what better way to do that than to travel. Travel broadens the mind and assists learning. Knowledge comes to you very quickly if you look and listen. In any event, person to person contact is vital, even in today's world of email, fax and mobile phone.

To summarize the key aspects of reducing your risk of failure when negotiating overseas, the following points should never be overlooked:

- Plan well ahead of travelling. Tiredness on arrival at a negotiation is not acceptable or productive for important discussions.

- Learn about the most important manners and customs of your hosts. If you do not, it is possible you will inadvertently cause offence, which will affect your ability to negotiate effectively. Above all, respect those manners and customs, however incomprehensible they may seem when compared to the way you live your life.

- Never comment on another country's politics, religion, way of life, ethics, judicial system, corruption, or matters which conflict with your personal preferences. Ultimately, you are there for business and as the "face" of your company.

- Smile, never show discourtesy, however irritated you may be with the way a negotiation is being handled by the hosts, and continue to show respect, both to your hosts and to other members of your team who may be struggling with the changed environment.

- If any aspect of the deal makes you feel uncomfortable, ethically or in respect of the business terms, remember that you always have the option to say "no". The fact that you have worked a long time for a deal or invested a lot in the negotiations and opportunity for business should not influence you if it is not in the long term interests of your company. A well developed sense of awareness and instinct will help you. Take contemporaneous notes of the events so as to justify your actions when you reach home. This may be necessary as people in the home office will see things differently than you from where they are sitting back home.

- Remember that doing business overseas should

not be treated any differently from business back home. Meet the terms of the contract you enter into just as rigorously as you would in a contract you execute back home in your own country. Follow up on any difficulties or problems encountered, and stay in touch throughout the lifetime of the deal as you were the party with whom the cordial relationship with your hosts was first established. It will be appreciated.

It can be seen from the above chapter that the impact of *people* on negotiations can be just as influential on the successful outcome of an opportunity as external factors. As we are often told, "you don't get what you deserve, you get what you negotiate". This is true, but what you are able to negotiate is however irrevocably tied into how you conduct yourself. That conduct should always include the following attributes: listen, watch, wait, and learn.

CHAPTER 6

THE BREAKDOWN OF TRUST, CORRUPT PRACTICES AND THE IMPACT ON YOUR BUSINESS

Without trust, nobody takes risks. Trust is so vital to the way business is done that it is not an overstatement to say that it makes the difference between success or failure, rich or poor.

A breakdown in trust was the fundamental cause of the 2008/09 financial crisis because financial institutions ceased to trust the solvency of other financial institutions and their ability to repay loans and debt. The breakdown in trust became so severe that it brought the whole monetary system within an inch of complete collapse.

The tipping point of the loss of trust can be traced to the declaration of bankruptcy of Lehman Brothers on 15th September 2008, marking the largest bankruptcy in US history. Throughout 2008, Lehman had been struggling to maintain liquidity in the face of huge losses in the subprime mortgage market, and immediately before the declaration of bankruptcy it became clear that the other banks and traders had lost trust in Lehman's ability to honor its debts. When it found itself unable to obtain credit to continue trading, bankruptcy became inevitable and an astonishing position was revealed of bank debt of $613 billion and bond debt of $155 billion against assets of only $639 billion.

Immediately following the bankruptcy filing, the Dow Jones Industrial Average experienced its largest one day point loss, and but for a bailout package agreed by the US, UK, and other western governments, the international monetary system would most likely have collapsed completely. The reality is that this breakdown came about because of a loss of trust between businesses.

The problem of trust goes even deeper. It is a primary reason why some countries are rich and others are poor. If you don't trust the people you are doing business with, you tend not to do business, and without doing business you can't create wealth. People need assurance that the other party to a business transaction is going to honor their obligations. Trust in modern western economies has evolved to the point where large amounts of credit has been, and still is, committed between complete strangers on the belief that it will be repaid, and this trust has essentially fuelled modern industry.

But a look at the 2009 Corruption Perceptions Index (CPI) gives a good indication of how a lack of trustworthiness or unethical conduct reduces wealth when business dealings lack honesty. Where businesses cannot rely on the legal or bureaucratic systems to support contractual obligations without resorting to bribery, the ability to create wealth across the economy is reduced. The CPI is a remarkably good list of how the wealth of countries has a direct correlation to trust and corruption.

The Corruption Perceptions Index is published annually by Transparency International (TI) and lists in a league table format the countries of the world according to the "degree to which corruption is perceived to exist among public officials and politicians". TI defines corruption as "the abuse of entrusted power for private gain". The most common form of corruption is bribery, which TI define as "the giving or receiving of money, a gift or other advantage as an inducement to do something that is dishonest, illegal or a breach of trust in the course of doing business".

The 2009 CPI shows that out of 180 countries covered by the CPI, only 49 scored 5.0 or above: to put the CPI scores in perspective, a score of 10.0 would indicate a bribe was never used as part of a transaction, whilst zero would indicate that a bribe was always a part of a transaction. So almost 70% of countries included in the 2009 CPI are more likely to require bribes as part of business dealings than not. For information, the 2009 CPI is attached as Appendix 1 at the end of this book.

There is no doubt that degradation of markets is closely aligned to the levels of bribery required to do business. So it can be seen that doing business in the highest ranked countries on the CPI (Denmark, New Zealand, Denmark, Singapore, Sweden and Switzerland all scored 9.0 or more) is likely to be far more straightforward than in the lowest ranked countries (Somalia being ranked lowest with a score of 1.1). As many studies have shown, there appears to be a direct link between high levels of corruption and low levels of direct foreign investment.

Indicators (such as provided by the CPI) of the likelihood of bribery and corruption being required as part of business dealings is vital for traders, and particularly those who trade around the world, as risk increases considerably when bribery and corruption are involved in deals.

Some people might take the view that any method by

which they can help themselves to secure a business contract and beat the competition for that job is just "part of life". Their view would be: so what if that contract was secured through some form of corruption or device which competitors knew nothing about? These practices are widespread in one form or another and have been going on for years, so why change now?

The problem lies in the consequences of what is done to secure a contract. Corrupt practices bring with them risks which can produce devastating consequences both individually and corporately. It is not just about breaking the law, but also about the effects on the reputation and future prospects of individuals and companies that conduct secret activities for gain which would not be accepted by the public if they knew about it. This is why corrupt practices are of course kept secret, and secrecy tends to produce relationships which are unhealthy, unstable and unenforceable.

The CPI is a good index because it is a "perception" index, and shows the perception in the minds of the wider public as well as businessmen of the impact of corrupt practices and how they will be treated. In the countries listed in the top half of the CPI, equality of treatment is generally considered by the citizens of those countries to be so obvious and important that the legal and bureaucratic systems support this concept. The law in those countries supports the concept of equal, fair and transparent competition and effectively prosecutes those that try and seek gain through unfair practices. As one moves down the CPI list, the likelihood of the legal, political and bureaucratic systems supporting the concept of eliminating unfair practices are reduced.

Even so, bribery in all its various forms is illegal in most countries around the world, even in the most corrupt, and the penalties should you break those laws are severe. The risk of getting "found out and punished" is simply greater in some countries than others. If found out, severe financial penalties may be imposed, the possibility of personal fines and imprisonment for responsible directors and managers, loss of export licenses, and removal from preferred bidders lists by government bodies and large companies who have rules of conduct which require that business is only conducted with companies and individuals who are considered trustworthy and of good reputation.

Some shocking examples of the consequences to individuals and companies of breaking the law will be given below. But it is worth remembering that once you are perceived as a bribe payer to acquire business or favors, you cannot pull back from this practice – it will thereafter be considered by bribe receivers as part of the normal course of business. This applies in the private lives of individuals as much as in their corporate lives.

You might think that you are so smart with the execution of your schemes that you are never likely to get caught. But revelations of such practices arise from many different sources – government investigations and commercial intelligence gathering, audits, competitors and even disaffected employees or bribe participants who become "whistleblowers". It is hard to keep such practices so secret that no one knows, and because of the inherently unstable nature of secrecy, it doesn't take much before some factor changes and the truth comes tumbling out.

The Organization for Economic Cooperation and Development (OECD) fights bribery in international business through its Anti-Bribery Convention. It has been incorporated into the laws of 37 countries which have signed up to the Convention and allegations of bribery can be reported to the relevant embassies for prosecution under the laws of the relevant country. A list of these countries can be found on the OECD website. As a result of the activities of organizations such as Transparency International, OECD, and the changing laws of the developed nations, public awareness of bribery is increasing.

A decade or two ago bid-rigging and bribery were understood to occur and were generally accepted, or at least tolerated, as methods by which contracts were won across the world; indeed in some countries bribes were even tax deductible items. This notion is becoming very much less acceptable now, as the public consciousness and awareness of fair practices increases, and consequently company ethics and accountability have risen. It is therefore far more likely that corrupt and unfair practices will be apprehended eventually, and prosecuted under the law. The risk involved with these practices is therefore far higher than in previous decades.

However, after so many years of winning contracts through bribery and corruption, why should anything change? What are the reasons why people should stop paying or receiving bribes? There are lots of reasons, apart from the obvious ones of fines and imprisonment under the law. Unethical conduct, and in particular bribery, stunts economic growth in developing countries, discourages foreign investment, reduces and wastes public money which should be used for public services, prohibits effective governance due to corrupt enforcement officials, reduces trust in the legal system of a country which cannot be relied upon by businesses to support contractual obligations and ensure fairness of justice, and reduces wealth creation.

Ultimately, every country should have the best interests of that country as a whole at the forefront of its goals and vision. However, the only way certain greedy, selfish individuals who are in positions of power in developing countries can be stopped from putting public money into their own private pockets is by the rich countries around the world ensuring that their own citizens and companies are punished for supporting such selfish individuals.

This is why the enacting of the UK legislation on bribery in April 2010 is a welcome step in the process of ensuring public funds in developing countries are used for the benefit of the citizens as a whole and do not fall into private hands. Many of the world's biggest development deals in developing countries around the world were built by companies from the rich western nations, so by focusing on the enactment of powerful bribery legislation in those countries, much of the bribery can be deterred through good preventative legislation. Britain has finally joined the growing band of rich western nations who are using legislation aimed at their own citizens and companies to prevent bribery and corruption taking place around the world.

The Bribery Act in the UK was long overdue. It has now become law, having received the Royal Assent on 8th April 2010, and essentially consolidates in one place all the existing laws on bribery and corruption as well as significantly extending the reach of the law. It is a well drafted piece of legislation and is even more extensive than the equivalent US legislation (the Foreign Corrupt Practices Act), which set the standard for extraterritorial reach in combating bribery and corruption for decades before other western countries started to catch up.

The law had four key components and they are easy to follow. It becomes an offence to bribe or to be bribed, it becomes an offence to bribe foreign officials, and finally it also becomes an offence for a commercial organization to fail to prevent bribery. This final offence takes the law beyond where the US legislation reaches, as the US legislation is limited to bribing foreign public officials and does not cover bribery outside of the government/public official arena. The defence to bribery for commercial organizations is that the commercial organization had adequate procedures in place which were designed to prevent persons associated with the commercial organization from undertaking such conduct. Until the UK Justice Secretary issues the guidelines, the legislation will not come into effect, but these guidelines are expected to be released during 2010.

This legislation, when it comes into effect, will materially help the Serious Fraud Office to combat corrupt practices, and gives it power on a par with the US Government. Corrupt dealings and practices are often complex, global operations, and this legislation was needed to allow the SFO to work more closely with other international agencies to effect "global settlements" with offenders around the world. Western companies have been the main practitioners globally of corrupt practices to influence commercial deals, with the citizens of developing countries being the main losers as a consequence. This legislation, alongside the US and other European nations legislation, such as in Germany and France, is a major global step to correcting this failing.

Before providing critical risk reduction methods for use in combating practices which create unlawful and unfair advantages, it is worth looking at some examples of individuals and companies who suffered the consequences of their actions. Examples have been taken from the USA, Germany, France, the UK, and a United Nations matter, but anyone wishing to do business in any country around the world can go onto anti-corruption websites and get helpful impressions of the way corruption is approached in that country – examples are plentiful. This chapter will however concentrate on a few cases that are clearly in the public domain and not simply allegations.

- Halliburton, Nigeria

During 2009, Halliburton agreed to pay the US government $559 million in fines to end the investigation into a former subsidiary, Kellogg Brown & Root, concerning its involvement in bribing Nigerian officials to obtain contracts relating to the construction of a liquefied natural gas export plant in Nigeria. An action had been brought under the US Foreign Corrupt Practices Act, and the fine paid was reportedly the largest fine ever paid to the US government relating to allegations of bribery. It also led to the dismissal of certain senior executives. It has also caused the subsequent filing of a shareholder lawsuit. The legal costs and management time expended, in addition to the fines actually paid, would have been substantial.

- Siemens, Germany

Following bribery investigations around the world, Siemens agreed to pay fines in the USA and Germany for accounting irregularities, and the costs in legal fees, fines, internal investigations and management time have allegedly exceeded $2billion. Siemens have apparently now put in place internal anti corruption measures, and the OECD believes that the Siemens case shows that practices such as bribery are being taken more and more seriously around the world.

- Elf Aquitaine, France

In November 2003, French courts sentenced three key executives at Elf Aquitaine, the well known oil company, to jail terms and large fines for using company money as bribes. The trial kept the French public riveted for months, and was described by one British newspaper as "perhaps the biggest financial scandal in western democracy since the end of the second world war". The company was subsequently privatized and is now run under different management.

- United Nations oil-for-food program

In 2007, a prominent US oil trader was sentenced to serve a jail term for violating rules of the United Nations program after admitting to making secret surcharge payments to enable his company to import Iraqi oil to the USA.

- United Kingdom

In August 2009, following a four year enquiry, the Office of Fair Trading announced that up to 112 construction companies would face fines for participation in an industry-wide practice known as "cover pricing", whereby companies would collude with each other and make high unattractive bids for public sector contracts, allowing work to be awarded to co-conspirators. The construction industry has now issued a new code of conduct to clean up its damaged reputation from questionable bidding practices, which leading construction companies have agreed to adhere to.

In May 2008, BAE Systems published an internal report into the company's ethical practices and agreed to implement its recommendations following a four year Senior Fraud Office investigation into bribery allegations in relation to a multi-billion pound contract in Saudi Arabia. In relation to other matters, BAE Systems also announced in February 2010 that it had reached settlement with the US Department of Justice and the UK Serious Fraud

Office relating to investigations which had stretched back as far as 2004, paying a fine of $400 million to the US Government and £30 million to the UK Government. BAE Systems stated ""These settlements enable the Company to deal finally with significant legacy issues. In the years since the conduct referred to in these settlements occurred, the Company has systematically enhanced its compliance policies and processes with a view to ensuring that the Company is as widely recognised for responsible conduct as it is for high quality products and advanced technologies." It can be seen that compliance with the law is imperative, as the consequences of failure to follow the law can have damaging financial consequences, and it is hoped that other companies follow the compliance process now being adopted by BAE Systems.

Whilst matters which reach the public eye may be relatively few and far between and tend to be eye-catching matters which the media pick up on in order to sell newspapers, there is an increasing appreciation of the risks associated with bribery, corruption and other unfair business practices, and the need to eliminate such practices. A good example is the August 2008 announcement by the Dubai Government that it expects complete transparency in business dealings following its decision to charge certain government officials with graft and embezzlement.

Risk assessment considerations

To ensure that companies manage this risk effectively, all companies should establish a code of conduct for business dealings to ensure ethical conduct applies when employees negotiate contracts around the world. Bribes in return for the award of contracts are normally made through the use of intermediaries such as agents, through local joint venture partners or local subsidiaries, or through subcontractors in countries where the law may be more lenient or where discovery of a commission payment may be less likely to be detected. Often bribes are paid with the knowledge of the senior management for the sole purpose of winning the contract, and no individual within the company benefits directly. The risk of discovery may therefore be unbalanced when considering the individual penalties that may be applicable on discovery, such as fines and imprisonment.

It is worth asking certain key questions as part of the risk assessment:

- In what countries are you doing business? The CPI league table will give you a good idea as to whether a particular country is a "red flag" country for bribery.

- Do you have any significant contact with government officials in those countries?

- Is your company's business overly dependent on those markets?

- How do you conduct your business in those countries? Through an agent or through company representatives?

- Is the business generated from those countries worth the potential fines and other penalties if bribery was discovered?

- Is reputational damage a factor that you would be concerned about if bribery was discovered?

Risk management methods:

Use of agents: where agents, sponsors or representatives ("agents") must be used in obtaining contract awards, (1) all agreements to utilize such persons should be in writing; (2) payments should be conditional on award of the contract; (3) compliance with the relevant bribery laws should be expressly required; (4) payments should be proportionate to monies received by the seller/contractor from the client; (5) no activity by the agent should be allowed before he has signed an agreement with the company as agents sometimes make claims later based on verbal discussions with a company salesperson if the proposed appointment falls through.

Due diligence: before committing to the use of an agent or representative to help the seller/contractor seek work in a particular territory, due diligence checks should be carried out on the agent, including such matters as whether the agent is related to government or political party officials, and his general reputation in the territory from the viewpoint of knowledgeable local persons or organizations of good standing. The company salesperson should be required to complete a due diligence check list for use by the company's management in approving the use of a particular agent, as this agent will usually be the "face" and point of contact on behalf of the company in the territory.

Business territories: A regular check should be kept on reports of the use of corruption in specific territories to win contracts, as this can act as a "red flag" to consideration of bidding for work in new territories where a contractor has not worked before.

Use of joint venture partners or subsidiaries: Contracts should be in place between the company and its partners or subsidiaries and all contracts should contain anti-bribery language, and effective checks and balances and controls should be in place between the joint venture partners before commitments are made.

Internal procedures: Proper procedures should be in place within a company for dealing with agents who may assist in the award of business in a foreign territory. Individuals within a company such as sales staff should never act in isolation, and should be subject to company "checks and balances" as set out in internal company procedures.

A final note of caution:

When individuals take personal risks on behalf of a company they should always bear in mind the following dictum:

"The rewards for success are immeasurably smaller than the penalties for failure".

Dismiss these words at your peril.

PART 2 – EVENTS

CHAPTER 7

RISK AND SUCCESS

Good Management of Risk Means Success

In all sectors of business, management of risk should be an integral part of a company's business model, and not just an exercise in meeting regulatory requirements.

To be successful requires the formulation and understanding of two things: (1) the objectives of the company and (2) the risks that the company may face in pursuing those objectives.

All companies should have key objectives, and the achievement of those objectives requires the effective management of risks that could reduce the company's ability to meet the key objectives.

Success is far more closely correlated to the management, control and reduction of those risks than is often acknowledged by a company's senior executives. However, as the occurrence of identified potential risk decreases, costs are reduced, less management time is spent firefighting, and this allows more time for management to focus on achievement of the key company objectives. This in turn normally causes increases in profitability and a greater likelihood that company objectives will be achieved. The reduction in "surprises" leads to greater shareholder confidence in the way the business is being run, and this in turn leads to a higher share value, and greater return on investment.

The above paragraph shows how the process of good risk management makes a company successful.

As in almost every aspect of life, finding a balance is important. In a competitive market economy, a company with a low risk appetite is unlikely to generate a high rate of return. However, excessive risk taking may cause complete company collapse, so finding optimum balance will generate the greatest return on investment. The question for management is whether their policy on risk leans towards avoidance and therefore lower profitability or, alternatively, greater risk taking which, if well managed, leads to greater profitability.

Some risks should be reviewed as corporate/group level risks and some as project level risks. Whether at corporate or project level, senior executives should consider:

(1) the kind of risks that may arise;

(2) whether as a corporate policy they are prepared to accept these risks;

(3) the likelihood of the risks materializing;

(4) the cost to limit the risk; and

(5) the ability of the internal policies and procedures to reduce the impact of a risk if it occurs.

Think risk. Making risk assessment a separate independent database from other existing management information systems is not going to help management understand risk. It is far better that risk assessment becomes part of the everyday thinking of management, and that way it becomes part of the culture of the company, and integral to existing management information systems. It is not helpful when executives see filling in forms related to risk as a "dreaded task" for addition to a database that may only be used to satisfy regulators, auditors, insurers and lawyers.

Everyone should be aware of risk, and understand how to manage risk. This requires, firstly, a knowledge of how risk management fits into the existing management information system, and secondly, an understanding of how important effective communication between different divisions and departments within a company is. These two factors drive the level of success a company has in controlling and reducing risk. Corporate/group level policies and decisions can only be made effectively at Board level if the upward communication to them contains sufficient data for them to make those policies and decisions objectively.

The human factor

Whilst a good risk management system should assist achievement of a company's objectives, there is however a "proviso". There is a risk factor which can still derail the risk management process, however well formulated. This is the risk attributed to *people themselves.* In other words, "people risk", as described in the first part of this book.

When analyzing the failure of a company to meet its objectives, the human factor should never be omitted. The possibility of poorly judged decision making, human error, deliberate circumvention of checks and balances and controls, and inappropriate reaction of individuals to external risk factors can never be eliminated completely from a company's risk management performance. This section of the book concerns the risk related to external factors rather than "people risks", but risk reduction must always take into account human actions and the impact of negative human traits. It can derail the best risk management policies and procedures.

Aside from the impact on a company's prospects of negative human traits as previously described, anyone entrusted with taking decisions about risk factors should always make those decisions *objectively*. The principles for assisting objective decision making related to commercial risk will be addressed later in this chapter, and those principles should assist in the elimination of the subjective aspects of decision making. Decision makers must eliminate their natural subjective bias based on culture, upbringing, training, or political leanings and concentrate on objective analysis.

Communication

As mentioned above, communication is a key factor in management's ability to make sensible decisions relating to the risk attached to a possible action or project to be pursued by the company.

The best circumstances for management decision making is where the executives have received all the required information to make a sensible decision. This would mean their decision making is being made with the benefit of *total certainty* and therefore can comfortably predict the likely outcome from the data available.

Certainty is not however often encountered in the cut throat world of business. Most decisions are in reality made without all the facts to hand, and so the outcome of the company's proposed course of action is not certain. The less data is available, the more uncertain the likely outcome is.

This is where risk analysis comes in, as management needs to be able to work out as far as possible whether taking a particular course of action is a "gamble" (because the upside or downside cannot be properly assessed) or whether a risk is manageable and assessable in terms of potential profitability or the possible loss which may occur.

If none of the potential risks associated with a particular course of action arise, then profit should be assured (if the data that management received is correct); but if an identified risk does arise, this is likely to lower profitability unless managed appropriately. Appropriate management of risk can only occur if risk principles for management of risk have been put in place at both corporate and project levels to reduce the impact of a possible adverse event, or better still, to eliminate the possibility entirely.

If an adverse future event occurs, it is always controlled best when planned for in advance rather than considering a solution after the event has already occurred. There are cost effective methods to reduce risk (which will be addressed later) related to an adverse event when planned in advance, but most solutions are costly if an event is not planned for. Impact of an event occurring should of course be viewed against the effect on the objectives set by the company.

Communication in control of risk is vital. One simple reason for the repetition of errors in different jobs by the same company is lack of communication. Communication helps people learn. The failure to make the most of the existing experience and resources within the company's organization will lead to the same type of errors being committed again and again. Failure to train newer staff adequately and communicate the wealth of knowledge available within a company and internal departments is a common failing, and junior or inexperienced employees should be encouraged to seek assistance from more experienced colleagues so that succession planning is aided and failures not repeated.

Younger staff should not fear asking questions. New employees with new ideas brought in from other companies should be recognized and encouraged. Finally, it is rare that a matter within a company is so confidential that it cannot be communicated within the company. Ill informed people spread rumors which are invariably damaging. Information removes fear, and managers should communicate directly with subordinates, not through needless intermediate stages. A well informed company is a productive, positive and enthusiastic company, and risk and mistakes will be reduced through good internal communication.

Objectives

Before considering the organizational structure for "checks and balances" in decision making, it is important for businessmen to understand clearly what the objective is behind every project they are considering undertaking. Key executives should not have different ideas on what the ultimate objective is – but it is surprising how often executives are not in fact "in tune".

For instance, if a Company was to engage in a new area of work, or projects in a new territory, the decision-makers should be clear on the key objectives. The following checklist questions would need to be answered to ensure key personnel have the same thinking:

1. Is the Company clear about the aims and objectives for the Company with respect to the venture: i.e. what is it trying to achieve in the short term (by the end of the first year) and the medium terms (second year, third year, fourth year).

2. Can the defined objective be achieved without consuming excessive management time and other resources to the detriment of other parts of the business of the Company.

3. Does the Company have sufficient human resources already available to meet the (yearly) objectives, or will further resources be required from outside the Company. If so, will this be possible, and at what cost.

4. What training will be needed to meet the objectives, and what will be the cost of "training" the in-house staff.

5. Will it be necessary to borrow money to achieve the (yearly) objectives. If so, has the cost been factored in, and are lines of credit available.

6. What is known about the competition in the market the Company is entering, and what does the Company understand or anticipate the competition is, or will be, doing. Are other companies successful in the market at the present time, or are they merely "surviving".

7. Are the projections for revenue realistic. How

have the projected revenue figures been reached. What assumptions have been made.

8. Have best case and worst case scenarios been projected.

9. Is geographic expansion realistically possible.

10. What permits/licenses will be required to allow the objective to progress.

The answers to these questions will focus key executive decision makers. If there are negative responses to any question, the venture needs reassessing, as the risk of loss on the venture will not have been properly assessed.

Internal Company Procedures

Management of risk necessitates control of internal company decision making. Most business managers would say they take precautions as a matter of routine when making decisions, such as assessing the chance of failure and finding ways to reduce the probability of failure.

Unfortunately, the "human factor" comes into play more often than managers would like to admit, for all the reasons outlined in Part 1 of this book. Reasoned decision making, based on following company procedures and checks and balances which most companies have in place to a greater or lesser extent, and which should be well known to managers, often disappears because of (1) time pressure: "the manager needs something done now"; (2) ambition and greed: "if this works I'll get noticed, get praised, get a bonus and maybe promotion"; (3) ego: "I know more than everyone else about this";

(4) complacency: "it has worked well before"; (5) lack of responsibility: "it's not my money".

Conversely, sometimes managers can find it hard to make decisions, constantly trying to delay the day when a decision has to be made by requesting more investigation, more data, until the opportunity has passed. There's always a good reason why delaying making a decision is appropriate, which can have the undesirable effect of limiting business growth.

The key is getting the right balance between taking decisions quickly but which are badly thought through, and delaying decisions whilst further security and certainty is sought, which may never arrive. Finding the balance is the basis of the system of "checks and balances" which every company should utilize.

Once the objective(s) of the company are clear, an organizational structure should exist for swift decision making backed up by proper checks and balances to ensure key risk principles are not overlooked.

Most companies generally issue contract policy procedures to ensure that:

1. Responsibilities and levels of authority are fully documented and understood throughout the organization;

2. The appropriate level of approval is obtained for all contractual commitments;

3. Adequate checks and balances to decision making are in place within the organization and critical decisions cannot be made without the knowledge and approval of others;

4. Business secured by the company is achievable without exposure to unacceptable risks, and at the same time returning an adequate and acceptable contribution to overheads and profit.

Procedures will normally require new business opportunities to be identified and developed by sales or business development staff, who will be located either in the company's headquarters offices or elsewhere domestically or internationally depending on the company's geographical spread of work.

Once an opportunity to submit a bid for work has been identified, the decisions as to:

(a) whether to submit a bid for the work and

(b) the final form and content of the bid to be submitted

will normally be taken by an internal company approval committee.

A manager to oversee the progress of the bid will be identified, as will resources to be utilized in putting together the terms of the bid, and the budget available for the bid, up to contract award. The resources utilized internally will include relevant members of the design, operations, pricing/estimating, finance, commercial, and legal/contracts departments. These personnel are necessary to ensure the bid is given proper consideration and adequate checks and balances are adhered to, to counter the natural desire of the sales staff to win the work at any cost.

It is important for a distinction to be made between major and minor value bids. This normally involves delegation of decision making within pre-determined financial limits. Often business decisions relating to a bid for work need rapid decisions, particularly when client/customer meetings occur, and bringing together senior staff or board members is not practical for every day decisions. Presentations at meetings involving executive summaries, visual aids and so forth where meetings consume vast amounts of the time of key executives simply is not practical. Routine decisions for transactions below an agreed financial figure are therefore delegated to an appropriate level of manager, possibly combined with a second signatory of a more senior level depending on financial authority limits. Decisions related to major high value bids or risks remain with senior management.

After contract award, be proactive.

Sometimes there can be internal friction about the conduct of a bid. However, regardless of the rights and wrongs that may have occurred between different departments during the course of a bid, once a project has been awarded, the execution or operations department should adopt a positive and proactive approach towards the execution of the work, in other words "take ownership" of the contract.

They need to put to one side any misgivings they may have concerning the terms of the contract that was negotiated and signed. Perhaps the contract could have been better negotiated, better terms obtained, but they must now live with what has been achieved and put the past behind them. Blaming people is negative and not constructive or conducive to a good end result. The sales team should continue to be involved during the life of the project (and as coordinated by those executing the work – it should be remembered that the relationships formed between the negotiators of the contract may help later on if problems arise).

If some of the terms were risky, the execution/operations team need to pay particular attention to these terms right from the start of the work. They should read the contract carefully before commencing execution of the work, understand its terms and act to reduce contract risk wherever possible. Even a "bad" contract can be helped by careful documentation and record keeping during project execution. It is difficult to maximize project income and revenues without this approach.

Successful development of a business requires a high degree of coordination between departments, and the organizational structure should permit this. There should always be flexibility of movement of personnel between departments to ensure appropriate teams are formed for bidding or execution of awarded work.

CHAPTER 8

RISK PRINCIPLES

There are certain principles relating to risk assessment which are worthy of consideration in all business deals. These principles all not always applicable to all parties in every deal, but should always be considered when looking at the risk that companies may be about to take on when they commit to a contract. They are high level, overriding principles rather than project specific or deal specific principles of risk analysis. Project or deal specific risk, and methods to control and reduce those risks and potential liabilities are addressed in a later chapter. These high level, overriding principles are as follows:

1. **Think "loss", not "profit".**

Many projects are unique, complex, and contain many inherent risks and opportunities to make losses.

It is far more appropriate therefore to set financial approval levels for executives that are based on how much a company can lose on a venture than on the likely price or value of a venture, or the projected profit. Small deals can produce big losses. This induces immediate financial prudence and forces executives to review their decision making in a realistic light. It forces them to look at the true risks and address the management or reduction of those risks so that those risks do not become a "surprise" later on in the event that they arise.

Profitability reduces as risks occur, but the cost is far more manageable if the executives understand and have addressed potential risks when bidding for work. Naturally, if risks do *not* occur or are avoided, profitability increases. Whilst it is always the aim of management to encourage conditions under which profit can be obtained, it is more important that a company's asset base is as healthy at the end of a project as at the time the company started the project. This is the essence of risk management – (as a minimum) to retain the company's asset base and reduce potential loss. Loss can only be sustained for limited periods before banks and shareholders lose faith in the company and its management and the continued viability of any investment. Losses cause companies to collapse. Management of risk to limit loss produces profit, as was shown at the start of Chapter 7.

From a commercial perspective therefore, the first rule of project analysis is not, as one might have expected, "how much money can I make on this project", it is in fact the reverse: "how much money can I lose on this project"? It is not the right approach for a salesman to say, without reference to other factors, "we must get this job". He should always say: "we must get this job on the right terms". He should be seeking the balance between risk and reward. It is important not to lose what the company has already gained, what it already has as cash and assets. Loss reducing principles are set out below. A company negotiator should always be prepared to say "no" to the offer of work where the terms of the contract leave him with too much risk of making a loss based on his analysis of these terms.

2. **Understand what you are agreeing to.**

Whilst this might sound like an obvious statement, it is remarkable how often negotiators arrive at business meetings without having prepared properly. Contracts are agreed and signed, and then some while later, an executive will say, "how can we have agreed to that provision"? This is not good for the long term health of a company. In the rush to finalize the deal, the negotiators may not have clearly established what the risks in a project are, may not have fully evaluated them, and consequently may well not be doing all that they can to limit the impact of those risks. Moreover, often they have not even read the contract properly, so they are unlikely to understand the significance of language, and perhaps will not realize as clearly as they should the impact of certain aspects of the deal, including how matters such as responsibilities and liabilities will operate.

Losses caused by not following the requirements of a contract occur far more frequently than they should do. It is surprising how often an analysis of how a loss occurred results in the conclusion that the terms of the contract were not adhered to by the persons who should have understood its terms precisely. Perhaps the manager responsible was overworked, had no time, or was focused on other matters.

He would hardly welcome the old saying "there's never enough time to do it right the first time, but time enough to do it over if it's wrong"! It is important to understand the written words that your company agreed to. In Chapter 9, key principles and presumptions relating to terms contained in contracts which affect risk and interpretation will be analyzed, and in Chapter 12 specific contractual issues, terms and conditions are also analyzed.

Although a manager will hopefully never simply "put the

signed contract in the bottom drawer of his desk and just get on with the job", because he should be constantly referring to it to ensure he is abiding by its terms (for instance in relation to any requirement for notifications to the other party that the contract may require), but he usually hopes he will not have to rely on the terms of the contract in a court of law.

However, how many projects reach their conclusion without some sort of dispute over time, money or other issues at the end of the project? It is therefore imperative that before a company enters into a deal, the participants are fully aware of what that deal involves. Put another way, there is only one time to get the contract terms right. That is before the contract is signed.

Share Risk

The concept of sharing risk is hardly new, but how risk is allocated between parties is a much harder matter to get right. Nobody wants to assume risk for any particular occurrence if they can pass that potential liability or monetary expenditure to cover the risk somewhere else. As a general rule, neither Buyer nor Seller should accept *all* risk in carrying out work. There should be a mutually agreeable sharing of the risk in carrying out the work.

Risk sharing on a contract or project is an equitable division or allocation of risks and liabilities among all the parties involved in a contract or project. The objective of risk sharing is to clearly and fairly define the rights and apportion the risks among the participants in the project, and with an end goal or objective of completing the project within budget, on schedule, and with a minimum of claims and litigation. The way this gets achieved most efficiently is by a fair allocation of risk among participants.

The problem is that it is often difficult to work out what a fair or equitable allocation should be. Those with the power and money want to keep their money and use their power to ensure that all liability rests elsewhere, but that is not necessarily a sensible course of action. A project owner, or powerful buyer, who may have vast wealth and resources, should share risk because it is the method by which they will most likely achieve their objective of completing a project on time, within budget, to the standards required, and without major disputes and difficulties.

A provider of services such as a contractor or supplier ("Service Provider"), generally speaking, tend to have relatively small asset bases compared with the project owner, and consequently tend to make small profit margins in undertaking the work. Clients and owners with strong balance sheets and asset bases should understand that companies with smaller asset bases view risk allocation differently and tend to look at five ways of dealing with risk:

- Price it

- Insure it

- Avoid it

- Contain it

- Share it

Pricing: If a Service Provider priced every possible risk, he would be unlikely to win many jobs. The pricing option is therefore limited by competition. There are some risks that have to be priced and provided for by contract or law, and the list of possible risks that can be identified will be considered later. The question for anyone trying to run a business and remain competitive is finding the balance between risk and reward.

Insuring: Insurance as the sole method for dealing with risk is not feasible, as insurance does not in itself limit the liability of a party, it only covers risks insured against, and only to the financial level agreed with the insurer. If liability arises at a level beyond the level covered by insurance, that liability remains the responsibility of the insured to pay. Further, should a risk materialize and the Service Provider makes a claim or claims on insurance policies, this is likely to increase premiums in future years both for the claimant and possibly the industry as a whole. It is therefore an expensive method of coping with risk that arises, assuming of course that the Service Provider in question can actually obtain suitable insurance cover at all in subsequent years. Insurance in any event does not, and cannot, cover every risk encountered by a party. Insurance is an area that appears simple but is widely misunderstood by executives. It is imperative when assessing risk transfer through insurance that persons that are well versed in insurance coverage are involved.

Avoiding: The avoidance of a big risk in the event that it arises is a "one time" solution. This is because it involves the liquidation of the company where the liability that arises exceeds the limits of the assets of the company that is liable for the risk. It is a rare contract these days though where a project owner allows a Service Provider to enter into a contract using a nominal value "off the shelf" company which has no asset base. Normally he will ensure that should a party enter into a contract using a nominal value or low value company, the company backs up its performance with suitable bank bonding, and parent company guarantees. Insolvency or liquidation of a company will damage the reputation of the Service Provider in the market, from which it may not recover. However, even if a Service Provider has provided guarantees to cover his performance, the occurrence of a large loss may nevertheless push a viable company into insolvency or even liquidation, and this can be disastrous for the Buyer or Developer as well.

Containing: Where a risk has been allocated to the Service Provider, and such risk is potentially unquantifiable in its effect, attempts should be made to contain the worst effects of such a risk. This requires the parties to a deal to negotiate limits on potential liabilities, and other methods of containing risk, examples of which will be considered and analyzed later.

Sharing: The most appropriate method therefore of dealing with risk is to share it, and agree between the parties an appropriate level of risk / liability for a project. If the parties equitably share risk, clients can be assured that if a problem arises in future years, the Service Providers will be in business to help solve the problem and to bear their share of the risk. The parties should share risk according to the party who is better able to manage or control that risk, but Service Providers only earn revenues and profit until the day they complete the work – owners of projects then start receiving revenues from the beneficial use of the product completed for years to come. Owners are therefore capable of sharing risk and amortizing their share of any liability or cost overrun which is incurred during the period of project development/construction/supply over many years thereafter. Risk can also be shared through joint venturing, partnering and subcontracting.

Companies that continually accept unlimited risks that they cannot insure or sustain will inevitably be forced to avoid losses through company liquidation or will be forced into insolvency. There are plentiful examples of parties that gambled with accepting high risk and failed. Some of these failures have been spectacular, with huge losses sustained on just one contract causing liquidation to occur in an otherwise healthy company. By being responsible in the risks that a company accepts, its salesman and managers are being good businessmen as well as being good at the work and services which is expected of them.

Limit Liability

The maximum level of financial liability that a company should accept when entering into a contract cannot be left unconsidered or unaddressed. In particular, a Service Provider should attempt to include a maximum overall limit of liability into the contract, or at minimum address limiting liability to a specific financial level for specified risks. In this way, in the worst case scenario, a Service Provider is aware of his "bottom line" risk if all goes wrong. Where no overall financial liability limits are agreed by the parties, the agreement of "sub limits" by addressing likely liability in specific areas of the contract, such as late completion, defective engineering or workmanship, pollution, and damage to people and property is helpful as this re-allocates and balances risk liability according to financial capability. Specific areas of risk such as those mentioned above will be examined in a later chapter – this chapter is simply clarifying the key principles.

Exclude liability for risks where the potential loss cannot be assessed

A company should never extend its potential liabilities into areas where the potential liability for a risk, if it should arise, cannot be assessed or quantified, and such risks should be excluded from the company's liability in a contract. A traditional area where liability is excluded because the potential extent of liability is unquantifiable is in relation to damages for indirect, consequential or economic losses. These are matters such as loss of profits, loss of revenues, loss of product, loss of production, and loss of future contracts or business. These losses can be devastating and cause business collapse for companies with limited asset bases if they are held or found liable for such losses. Regardless therefore of whether performance was poor and caused difficulties for the end user or buyer, liability must be excluded if at all possible. Some potential costs or damages directly associated with these failings can be assessed, and where they can, insurance against these risks can often be obtained at reasonable rates. What is not assessable however is a client's economic loss from these events, where the client loses revenues or profits due to reduction, or loss, of product, or reduction, or loss, of use of the facilities, possibly through interruptions and/or delays in production or lower output or throughput. Exclusion of such liability is simply about business survival.

Don't "bet" the company on any single contract or group of contracts

As mentioned earlier, it is possible to put a financially healthy company at risk through the acceptance of unbalanced contract terms on just one contract. This is where the "checks and balances" to internal decision making are vital to a company's health. There is a natural "tension" between individuals on behalf of a company who are selling and individuals who are thereafter required to operate or execute what the salesman has concluded in his contract negotiation. Decisions need to be made on bids where disputes exist between executives, and a decision-maker must be available to adjudicate between executives, which is likely to be a nominated individual under company procedures, all the way up the internal company chain to the Managing Director, or equivalent, depending on the size of the bid and risks involved. Where the system of "checks and balances" breaks down, as has been mentioned earlier in this book, the company may potentially be putting itself fatally at risk.

CHAPTER 9

CONTRACTS, COURTS AND BUSINESS 'GAMBLES'

The following contractual principles and presumptions are a useful guide when analyzing the way a contract has been written. Risk can be associated with words, or sometimes lack of words. The words used in contracts are interpreted in certain ways, and the language used can help or hinder the clarification of intention and the risk a party is liable for.

Additionally, executives signing contracts which are governed by or construed in accordance with English Law or in legal systems which are based on the English common law legal system should be particularly aware of these contractual principles and presumptions.

The principles and presumptions are as follows:

- If the contract language is clear and unambiguous, the courts will not vary the terms, even if the terms appear entirely unreasonable for one of the parties.

- If a contract has been badly drafted and the words used are unclear, the courts will look at the intention of the parties to decide what the parties meant when they used particular words, but will not change a deal if the intention is reasonably clear from the language.

- In deciding what the intention of the parties was, they will look at the commercial background in which the deal was agreed, and the presumption is that the parties did not intend to reach an unreasonable deal, and that the deal should be based on commercial fairness or business commonsense.

- Courts will only allow terms to be "implied" into a deal (in circumstances where they have not been written specifically into the deal) if such an "implied" term would "go without saying". The nature of the term would have to be such that it was obviously intended by the parties to apply.

- Silence in a contract is not a prudent way to address risk. Where the parties have not expressly stated their position, the law will apply and specify how any dispute between the parties is to be resolved, and this may produce a result that the parties did not intend.

- If work is commenced without a signed contract, make sure at absolute minimum that the key terms are written down and accepted by the parties when the work starts.

- There is a presumption against gambling by businessmen in contracts on the basis that businessmen generally do not make wild gambles such as unknown, unpredictable or unlimited liability.

The presumption against 'gambling'

The concept of taking a business 'gamble' has led parties

into the law courts, and has been addressed by the courts on many occasions. Ending up at the end of a venture with a dispute is never how you envisaged the situation when you started out, but it is worth understanding some of the basic principles and presumptions that may be utilized should your deal come "unstuck". This helps to better understand risk in signing complex contractual documents.

The starting point therefore is to understand how the courts view business 'gambling'. What judges do when such a case comes to court is to examine in detail the "small print" of the terms of complex contract documents. They do this in order that they may decide whether those terms of contract included a wild gamble by one company when entering into a contract (leading to large profits or large losses by that party), or whether the risks inherent in the deal were intended to be more appropriately allocated between the parties in the event of an adverse turn of events during performance of the work.

General principles related to the words used in contracts will be analyzed below, but the presumption against businessmen entering into 'gambles' needs addressing in the context of the common law legal system.

As a 'proviso' to any businessman thinking that 'gambling' in business is acceptable and is supported by the law, it should be remembered that courts do *not* vary the terms of deals, however wild, risky and commercially unsound, if the contract terms are clear and unambiguous, or if the parties knew the arrangement was a bet or "gamble" by one or both parties.

Many contracts around the globe utilize and reference the English common law system and English Law and its dispute resolution systems. In this system, judges create 'precedents' when deciding cases, and one of those precedents has been that there is a presumption against "gambling" in business deals which come before the English courts and are subject to English law. Many international disputes utilize the English legal system because of its known fairness, predictability and judicial independence.

A good example of the application of this principle came up in 1984, when in a well known shipping case, it was stated in the landmark judgment, (in relation to a clause in a bill of lading purporting to impose on the consignee an unknown, unpredictable and unlimited liability for demurrage) the following:

"I venture to assert that *no business man who has not taken leave of his senses would intentionally enter into a contract which exposed him to a potential liability of this kind*, and this in itself, I find to be an overwhelming reason for not indulging in verbal manipulation of the actual contractual words used [in the charterparty] so as to give them this effect [when they are treated as incorporated in the bill of lading]".

The key words are highlighted, and set out the basic presumption.

Two years later, those words were echoed again in a complex case involving the Hong Kong Government and a major Japanese contractor (the "Mitsui case") relating to the construction of a large tunnel where millions of dollars were at stake over who should be liable for the cost overruns related to the work, which had cost far more than originally estimated. There it was stated in the judgment:

"it seems somewhat improbable that a responsible public authority on the one hand and responsible engineering contractors on the other hand, contracting for the execution of public works worth many millions of dollars, *should deliberately embark on a substantial gamble.*"

Again, the basic presumption is highlighted.

In that case, although a contract price had been estimated based on certain assumptions relating to the anticipated ground conditions and the quantity of materials that were estimated to be likely to be used in completing the work, the anticipated ground conditions were not what was revealed when the contractor started working. The parties both accepted that the nature of the ground through which the tunnel was to pass could not be accurately predicted in advance, and would only become known as excavation proceeded. As it turned out, the cost to complete the works was far higher than the original 'estimate'. The contract terms signed by the parties were very complex and technical and made allocating risk for the cost overrun unclear.

It was decided therefore that *as those terms were not absolutely clear* on who took the risk of the cost overrun if different conditions were discovered from those anticipated, the presumption was confirmed that the engineering company had not intended to take a 'gamble'.

Contract Language

Allocation of risk in the contract should be clear and unambiguous. This is so even when both parties to a contract use English as their first language, but in view of the fact that many international contracts are executed utilizing English as the language of the contract but with a governing law which is not English Law, uncertainty about the meaning or ambit of a term can itself be a major source of risk.

In understanding how the language of contracts can cause risk to a party, the following issues should be noted:

Bad Contract Drafting

A major problem in many deals is bad contract drafting, which can make understanding the true deal significantly more difficult. It is surprising that more contracts don't end up in complete disaster bearing in mind the lack of clarity that can often be seen in documents that companies sign.

A fundamental principle that practitioners all over the world should heed was emphasized in the Mitsui case referred to above:

This is that the *intention of the parties* must be ascertained *from the language they have used*, interpreted in the light of the relevant factual situation in which the contract was made.

The fact that a contract has been badly drafted doesn't change the rules on how language should be viewed and interpreted. Courts and judges aren't there to help overcome hurdles in interpretation imposed by poor quality drafting and to attribute to the parties an improbable and un-businesslike intention. If the language used, whatever it may lack in precision, is reasonably capable of an interpretation which attributes to the parties a precise intention, *then that is unlikely to be varied by the courts.*

Intention and Commercial Fairness

So how do courts interpret intention? Another judge, Lord Reid, in a case relating to a distributorship agreement for German machine tools, where the German manufacturing company wished to terminate the agreement for a trivial breach by the seller, stated as follows:

"the more unreasonable the result, the more unlikely it is that the parties can have intended it, and if they do intend it, the more necessary it is that they shall make the intention abundantly clear".

What he was saying was that if the parties knew when they were negotiating the contract exactly what they intended the basis of the deal to be, what the essential and fundamental terms were, *then they needed to write it down clearly and precisely.*

The problem is that, in putting the agreed "deal" between the parties into writing, often the basis of the deal becomes unclear from the language, and the courts are forced to interpret what the true deal was intended to be between the parties. So the Courts have worked out some useful principles for the application of 'intention', the primary principle being as follows:

They look at what is commercially fair and the commercial background to the contractual deal.

As was stated in the judgment in a 1998 case relating to a Swiss importer of sugar and a Bangladeshi company, in a dispute over a request for payment (a "call") being made on a bank bond:

"The court must have regard to the *commercial background, the context of the contract and the circumstances of the parties*, and to consider whether, against that background and in that context, to give the words a particular or restricted meaning, would lead to an apparently unreasonable and unfair result".

The judgment went on to state that the overriding principle in interpreting unclear drafting as to what the basis of the deal between the parties was intended to be, must be to maintain the *"balance of commercial fairness"* between the parties.

This concept of commercial fairness is now considered far more important than any other way of interpreting unclear drafting.

The judgment further stated that "a balance must be struck between the parties based on reason, fairness and commercial good sense".

Emphasis on *commercial fairness and common sense* in interpreting contractual language is repeated time and again in modern judgments. Again, in a well known shipping dispute (the "Antaios") it was held that if the literal meaning *was going to lead to a conclusion that flouts business commonsense, business commonsense has to take precedence*. The judgment followed previous cases where the language has to make good commercial sense.

A meaning that "imposed a financial liability of unknown extent that no businessman in his senses would be willing to incur" is not likely to find favor except where you simply can't avoid that conclusion. This principle is addressed immediately below.

Clear and Unambiguous Language

If however, the terms drafted into the contract are clear and unambiguous, the court will not, and cannot, either rewrite a contract or impose on the parties to a contract what the Court may think would have been a reasonable contract.

As was said in a defining case on clarity of words (on this occasion relating to the construction of a hospital nearly half a century ago):

"The Court does not make a contract for the parties. The Court will not even improve the contract which the parties have made for themselves, however desirable the improvement might be. The Court's function is to interpret and apply the contract which the parties have made for themselves. If the express terms are *perfectly clear and free from ambiguity*, there is no choice to be made between different possible meanings: *the clear terms must be applied* even if the Court thinks some other terms would have been more suitable."

So make sure you understand what you are writing down.

Implied Terms.

"Implied terms" have long been utilized to assist meaning and intention in written contracts. They are important to understand. An implied term is a term that "goes without saying". In other words it is a term which, if at the time the contract was being negotiated, someone had said to the parties: "what will happen in such and such a situation", they would both have replied "of course, so and so will happen; we did not trouble to say that; it is too clear." In other words, a term cannot be implied if there is doubt about the term. In essence, the term gives business efficacy to a contract.

It is not however advisable to leave the meaning to be worked out by a court of law, it is much better to draft it clearly and specifically into the contract. Why leave a term to the fate of a court? Reduce the risk of a decision going against you in court, and the cost of the case, by having clear, understandable language in the contract in the first place.

Surrounding Circumstances

Where language expressed in a contract is not clear, the courts often look at the "surrounding circumstances" to assist in interpreting the terms of a written agreement and understanding the intentions of the parties.

The court will look in particular at the objective(s) of the parties at the time they completed the deal. In reviewing the terms of a commercial contract, the Courts would certainly want to know the commercial purpose of the contract and the best way to find this out is to gain knowledge of the genesis of the transaction, the background, the context, and the market in which the parties are operating. This is the process of informing oneself of the "surrounding circumstances". However, it is not usual to refer to ongoing negotiations or preliminary drafts of contract documents between the parties in working out what the parties intentions and objectives were, as it is only the final version of the contract document which can be said to contain the consensus on all the issues reached between the parties.

Reasonableness is always a factor in assessing intentions anyway. A case that went all the way to the highest courts in England, the House of Lords, this comment was made: "when one is speaking of aim, or object, or commercial purpose, one is speaking objectively of what *reasonable persons would have in mind in the situation of the parties.*"

Unfortunately "reasonableness" is increasingly being

interpreted differently as society changes, so it is far better not to leave the outcome of a dispute in the hands of someone else (in this case a judge or arbitrator), far better to be clear about your intentions in the first place.

Conclusion on Language Interpretation: Commercial Fairness

In summarizing the interpretation of contract language that is unclear, the key issue when trying to work out how a court might view the deal you concluded, is to ascertain what is likely to be considered commercially fair and reasonable and makes common sense.

In coming to that conclusion, you need to be realistic, and not stretch the meaning of words.

Think in terms of the most obvious and natural conclusion based on the facts, background and context in which the deal was finalized, because this is the most likely conclusion of the judges should the matter end up in court.

Silence on risk in the Terms and Conditions of Contract

The objective of any contract should be to explicitly spell out each party's obligations, rights, and remedies in the performance of the work. This makes subsequent interpretation of the agreement easier in the event of a dispute. All provisions, clauses or statements contained in a contractual agreement are important. Conversely, where the contract is silent on an issue, this does not mean the issue is unimportant, or that there is no responsibility or liability in respect of the matter. When a contract is silent on a matter, the applicable law will determine what are the rights or liabilities of the parties.

Under many common law systems including English

law, in the absence of express words in the contract, the risk of completing the works for the price agreed, and overcoming all risks in doing so tends to rest with the party performing the work. So if you say "I'll do this work for a particular price by a particular date", but say nothing else, and the buyer agrees with that price and date, then all risks primarily rest with the seller. A seller of goods or services should always therefore try to state explicitly the position they wish to adopt on an issue, as the position that may be revealed by relying on the law may be far less favorable than a negotiated position. This is particularly important in the case of issues which, if they came to pass, could financially break the company. In carrying out the risk assessment of a potential deal you are thinking of entering into, make sure any issue which could break the company is not left silent in the contract you sign.

The essence of risk management should always be to know and understand the deal that has been reached, and leave nothing to chance, or which cannot be controlled, covered, or managed.

Commencing work without a Contract

It is advisable not to commence any work unless:

- a written contract has been signed by an authorized signatory of the Seller/Supplier/Contractor and the Buyer/Client; or

- an acceptable letter of intent has been signed by the Seller/Supplier/Contractor and the Buyer/Client.

An acceptable letter of intent is an instrument which

properly authorizes the Seller/Supplier/Contractor ("Seller") to commence work on all or part of the scope of work contained in the Seller's bid. Critical features that should be included in a letter of intent prior to acceptance and commencement of work (as this helps both the Seller and Buyer) are:

(a) a clear definition and understanding of the scope of work that the Seller is authorized to commence work on;

(b) a clear definition and limitation of the Seller's liability whilst performing work under the letter of intent;

(c) a clear commitment by the Buyer/Client for timely reimbursement for all work performed by the Seller under the terms of the letter of intent;

(d) a clear understanding of any limits on the Seller's authorization to spend (in other words, those costs incurred by the Seller for which the Buyer/ Client will be liable to pay for);

(e) agreed terms and conditions for performance, preferably including any terms that the Seller included in his bid.

Starting Work where the Final Price is Uncertain

Where certain key terms, in particular the price of the work to be carried out, are undecided at the time the Buyer/Client requests the Seller to proceed with the works pending finalization of the relevant key issue such as the price, the Seller will be entitled to recover a reasonable sum for work undertaken in the event that the parties ultimately fail to agree the price or any other key term which may affect the price.

This is called a "quantum meruit" payment. "Quantum meruit" is the right to be paid a reasonable remuneration for work done. The concept is that one party should not be enriched by receiving a benefit at the expense of the other party (the principle of "unjust enrichment").

The amount payable will however depend on the facts and intentions, but the basic principle applied by the courts is that the Seller should receive, so far as reasonably possible, the remuneration he would have received had the parties concluded the contract.

It is however preferable, if not imperative, that a Seller has a clear understanding of how he is going to be paid, preferably through the signing of a letter of intent, where he is asked to proceed with the work before he has concluded a contract. It is never a good idea to have to get the courts to decide what a reasonable price for the work should be, as going to the courts is costly and time consuming for both parties, and the result is out of your control.

An "Agreement to Agree"

Although it is possible to leave agreement of the final price to be agreed later on when the work is proceeding and the scope of work is clear, for the reasons stated above, other fundamental terms cannot be left open on the basis that they will be agreed later. Until those fundamental terms are agreed, there can be no contract in existence. "Agreements to agree" are essentially unenforceable in the courts.

The problem with ending up with an unenforceable contract is that one party may end up getting underpaid and one party getting unjustly enriched, or the application of the law reaching a result that was not intended by the parties.

It is imperative therefore that before any work is commenced, a properly agreed contract or letter of intent which agrees all the fundamental terms is concluded.

Bidding for Work

If a Seller wishes to object to any provision in the Client's bid documents, this should be addressed specifically in the Seller's bid for the work opportunity. If the Seller doesn't like the terms proposed by the Client but doesn't want to address every clause specifically in his bid, he must at least include a general qualification that his bid requires the parties to agree mutually acceptable terms and conditions in relation to certain issues before the work commences.

It is important to specify any very important terms which the Seller does not agree with from the Clients bid documents, as experience has shown that it is extremely difficult, if not impossible, to raise new issues at the negotiating table. The Seller may end up being required to accept a contract with unacceptable terms which he has committed to in his bid which he would prefer to walk away from. In tenders for public sector works, the Buyer is also increasingly bound by public sector procurement rules which limit negotiation and dictate that contracts must be awarded in particular ways. This may mean that a Seller cannot object to the Buyer's proposed terms.

He must therefore understand those terms clearly before he bids, as once the Client accepts his offer to carry out the works, the Seller cannot withdraw without a potential claim for damages by the Client for non-performance. If the Seller submitted a bank bond with his bid, this could also easily end up being cashed by the Buyer.

Conclusion

To emphasize the key contractual principles which can help reduce risk, as mentioned at the beginning of this chapter, remember:

- If the contract language is clear and unambiguous, the courts will not vary the terms, even if the terms appear entirely unreasonable for one of the parties.

- If a contract has been badly drafted and the words are unclear, the courts will look at the intention of the parties to decide what the parties meant when they used particular words, but will not change a deal if the intention is reasonably clear from the language.

- In deciding what the intention of the parties was, they will look at the commercial background in which the deal was agreed, and the presumption is that the parties did not intend to reach an unreasonable deal, and that the deal should be based on commercial fairness or business commonsense.

- Courts will only allow terms to be "implied" into a deal (in circumstances where they have not been written specifically into the deal) if such an "implied" term would "go without saying". The nature of the term would have to be such that it was obviously intended by the parties to apply.

- Silence in a contract is not a prudent way to address risk. Where the parties have not expressly stated their position, the law will apply and specify how any dispute between the parties is to be resolved, and this may produce a result that the parties did not intend.

- If work is commenced without a signed contract, make sure at absolute minimum that the key terms are written down and accepted by the parties when the work starts.

- There is a presumption against gambling by businessmen in contracts on the basis that businessmen generally do not make wild gambles such as unknown, unpredictable or unlimited liability.

The golden rule is always to understand what you are agreeing to before you sign. Read the terms of contract and make sure you understand what is written. If the language is not clear, then it is better to clarify it before you sign. Afterwards you must leave your fate in the hands of the law and the courts, and the rules and presumptions indicated above may apply.

CHAPTER 10

RISK IDENTIFICATION, CONTROL, ALLOCATION AND REDUCTION

Most industries have developed check lists of regularly encountered events where there is a risk of loss or damage should the event occur. These lists are used to identify potential risks and ideally allow management to categorize the events into high risk and low risk of occurrence, and the likely value of loss or damage based on the facts and circumstances that may be encountered.

Identification of Risk

Sources of risk tend to fall into the following general categories where change or uncertainty in the identified source of risk may affect a company's profitability or ability to meet its objectives:

- **Political**: change or uncertainty in government policy, or laws and regulations and difficulties in obtaining government permits and approvals;

- **Technical**: design adequacy of structures or systems, state of the art development issues, operational efficiency, and reliability of programs, products and installations;

- **Planning**: difficulties/delays in permission requirements, changes in policy, laws and regulations, unanticipated public opinion or objections;

- **Market**: changes in fashion or demand for a product, unexpected competition or competitor issues;

- **Environment**: changes in environmental laws and regulations, unexpected issues related to pollution or contamination, impact of public opinion on activities, government or regulatory authorities action or orders which affect anticipated costs or cause delays, unforeseen ground conditions;

- **Financial**: Changes in the cost of components, materials, labor or suppliers/contractors, failure of suppliers to perform, cash flow impacts, insolvency/liquidation of your company or others, margin reduction, underfunding of ventures or projects;

- **Economic**: changes in taxation, inflation, changes in interest rates or exchange rates, inability to obtain insurance for risks;

- **Force Majeure**: occurrence of events beyond the control of your company, such as war, weather, earthquakes, riots, closures, strikes, terrorism;

- **Personnel**: error, incompetence, negligence, lack of knowledge or experience, lack of training, lack of communication or instructions, tiredness, cultural difficulties, language, changes in labor regulations or conditions;

- **Safety:** changes in regulations, injury or death through collapse, accident;

- **Criminal**: theft, fraud, corruption, vandalism, lack of security;

- **Project**: unexpected changes or modifications required, and any project specific factor from the above categories;

By utilizing the check list that your company has formulated for risks in the industry it operates in, assessments can be made as to the severity and frequency of a potential loss, and the manageability of the risk.

Manageability of risk involves either:

- **Acceptance** of the risk as the risk assessment undertaken indicates that the company can absorb the impact of the risk through its own resources;

- **Transferring** the risk partially or fully to another party through insurance or through joint venture or partnering;

- **Eliminating** the risk through contract negotiation so that the responsibility or liability for the risk rests with another party; changing the approach so that the issue is avoided; or alternatively devising an exit strategy from the applicable venture so that the risk can be avoided and cannot affect your company or cannot impact the company should the risk materialize;

- **Controlling** the risk by effective procedures which reduce the impact of the risk event;

Transferring and eliminating risks are analyzed in more detail below. Controlling risk was dealt with in an earlier chapter.

Transferring Risk

Methods of risk transfer referred to in the above paragraph are analyzed in more detail below.

1. Insurance

The purchase of insurance to cover the possibility of an event occurring which could cause loss or damage to an organization is the most usual way of transferring risk. Some events are easier to insure than other events, some events require high value insurance and some only require low value insurance, and some events are uninsurable and so require government or self insurance. If an event is uninsurable, the contract must effectively eliminate this risk from the responsibility of the company. Uninsurable risks can range from nuclear or war risk, to certain environmental or political risks.

Insurance may become unavailable or too expensive from time to time, and it should be remembered when accepting responsibility and liability for a risk in a contract, which is then transferred to an insurance company through the purchase of an insurance policy to cover that risk, that insurance can cease to be available during the course of a contract or project, as it comes up for renewal intermittently, and sometimes insurance companies simply withdraw coverage.

Should a company decide to purchase insurance to cover a risk, the executives of that company should always remember that insurance is an asset of the company. It should therefore be treated with care. Many business negotiators see insurance as a "marketing" tool for helping to win work or new deals for their company, particularly where they readily allow other parties to be added as insured parties under the insurance their company has bought, without understanding that should a claim be made on that insurance policy, it may not be as readily or cheaply available when the policy comes up for renewal, as the claim will be registered as a loss against the record of that company, not the client.

Insurance policies should always be protected from the ability of parties other than the owner of the insurance policy from claiming on it. Parties often wish to be "added" as an insured party to an insurance policy purchased by someone else, but this is a risk which should be avoided if at all possible.

Some common sense rules for protecting a company's asset of insurance from use by others are set out below:

- Avoid adding other parties as "additional insured" to your company's insurance policies. As mentioned above, insurance is an asset and a company purchases insurance to protect the company itself from the occurrence of certain risks, not others. Access to this valuable asset should therefore be considered very carefully, and should never be allowed without appropriate financial recompense, if at all.

- If a party requests to be added as an additionally insured party under an insurance policy, that party should be asked why they need access to someone else's insurance. It is likely to be simply that it will enable that party to claim on someone else's insurance policy should an event arise, and will enable that party's own insurance policy to be insulated against a claim. Let's assume your company is asked by a client to allow the client to add his name to your insurance policy in the event of damage to the client's property or loss of data he possesses. If the client caused the loss or damage himself, there is no reason why your insurance policy should cover damage through the client's own fault.

- Always confirm with your insurance company that they are willing to allow another party to acquire rights to claim under your policy before you give that party the right. Adding a party as an additionally insured party under your insurance policy is likely to restrict the rights of your insurance company from seeking reimbursement from the other party (who caused the claim on the policy) as rights of subrogation from your company to your insurance company are unlikely to exist.

- If a party is added as an additionally insured party under your company's insurance policy, charge that party for the privilege of being an additionally insured party under your insurance policy.

- The extent of the additional insurance coverage should be limited in the contract to a specific amount per occurrence; a specific amount in the aggregate; a specific period of time; and as limited and specific a scope of coverage as possible.

- The contract should be precise and specific about what insurance coverage is being provided. Coverage requirements in the contract should never specify that a company is to provide "not less than" or "a minimum of" a specific level of coverage, as if your company has higher amounts of coverage than the contractual requirements, the other party gets access to all the coverage rather than the minimum required level. Let's say your company holds $100 million of coverage against a certain risk, but is only required to provide coverage under the contract for the other party of $5million. Then you should ensure that the other party only gets access to $5million of coverage, not $100million.

- If at all possible, do not provide copies of your actual insurance policies to any other party, as this information should remain confidential to your company. This is even more important if you have limited the other party's level of access to your company's insurance policy.

- Insurance coverage in a contract should be carefully aligned with contractual liability and any indemnities provided in a contract. When drafting a contract, insurance, liability and indemnities should flow together and not conflict with each other. For instance, if a company has negotiated with a client that the company will only be liable for damage or loss to the client's employees or property up to a specific figure, and the client has indemnified the company against liability above this specified figure, the company should only provide insurance up to the specified figure and no higher, even if the company has insurance at a higher level. Sometimes a company may include the client on its insurance policy and fail to limit the level of the client's access to the policy, so even though the liabilities and indemnities in the contract are clear, the insurance overrides the contractual limits thereby ruining all the good negotiating work that the executives of the company had achieved.

Joint Ventures

Joint ventures, whether in relation to a one-off project or a new business line, are an important method of reducing and transferring risk to others. A joint venture is a business alliance usually of limited duration formed by two or more unrelated businesses or professional entities for a particular purpose in which the skills, know-how and resources of the participants are combined.

The commercial arrangements for the joint venture vary from deal to deal, but will normally entail the sharing of costs, profits and losses. Where bidding for projects or entering new markets is very competitive and costly, it is not unusual for players in a particular industry to join together to share the risks or "downside" of an opportunity and similarly to share in the upside as well. All joint venture arrangements will be covered by lengthy and often complex contractual documentation, which deal with financial matters such as banking and bonds, liability and responsibility issues, decision making, approvals, and resolution of deadlock issues, the extent and scope of the participation of the parties, and many other matters such as confidentiality and legal issues.

Sometimes parties will come together for a one-off specific project opportunity under a "consortium" arrangement whereby scope of services provided by the parties is strictly separated, as are profits and losses. Each party in a consortium tends to control its own scope of services, and does not look to others for assistance. The main purpose of such an arrangement is to satisfy the requirements of a client, whilst at the same time limiting exposure of any one party to the complete risk attached to a project, particularly where that party does not have expertise in all areas of the project opportunity. Contractual and legal documentation will be similar to joint venture documentation, though it is less likely than in the case of a joint venture that a new company would be incorporated for the opportunity. Consortium partners often continue to use their own companies rather than set up new ones.

For a longer term strategy in a particular field of activity, collaboration of two companies may be more cost effective and reduce potential risk rather than the process of acquiring or merging with a competitor. Joint ventures offer the opportunity to share resources and know-how at far lower cost.

Such a strategy would usually involve:

1. Joint venturing with a key competitor.

2. Identifying a specific territory where the key competitor has influence and where working together in the territory (or territories) would be effective.

3. An aim to increase market share.

4. The sharing of profits with the key competitor from the expected increased market share.

5. The reduced cost of bids, operating expenditure and other costs.

6. The pooling of equipment and people to increase usage, and return on investment.

7. The ability to access a wider list of talented and experienced people for projects – clients tend be happier when they know that the people involved in the joint venture activities are the best available.

8. Increasing specific market knowledge, local contacts and know-how, as one day the joint venture may be broken up.

A joint venture structure would usually entail:

1. The setting up of a joint venture company, with the contribution of initial share capital and working capital, and agreement on such things as shareholding percentages.
2. Agreement on the zone to be covered by the joint venture.
3. Exclusivity of the work and services to be undertaken by the joint venture.
4. Agreement on the structure and management of the joint venture operations.
5. Use of an executive committee for key decisions.
6. Agreement of bidding and contracting philosophy.
7. Agreement on any equipment to be included from the parties as part of the newly-formed joint venture equipment.
8. Agreement on bonding, accounting procedures, insurance requirements, indemnity arrangements, and distribution of profits and sharing of losses and liabilities.
9. Consolidation of existing marketing arrangements, including consolidation of sponsors, representatives, and agents in the zone of the joint venture.
10. Responsibility for legal filings for anti-trust considerations as necessary.
11. Agreement for the provision of management and operational services and human resources.

2. Partnering

Partnering is also a method of sharing risk, between a company and its client rather than between competitors, as would tend to be the case with strategic project specific or long term joint venturing or consortium arrangements. Partnering is also undertaken either on a project specific or long term basis.

Partnering (sometimes called an "alliance") can give clients the benefit of lower costs and greater cost certainty. Improved co-operation between the design and implementation teams should also lead to an end product that is more specifically geared towards the client's needs. Additionally, there is greater chance of solving and resolving disputes between the company and its client without use of the legal process, as there should be a greater willingness within the joint partnering team to resolve design, on-site, personnel, vendor/supplier and subcontractor management issues and other problems such as cost increases, and delays, as the level of communication between the parties should be far closer.

The focus on setting common goals, sharing resources and solving problems together without resorting to the legal process applies just as much to a short term partnering arrangement as in a long term arrangement.

Whilst the precise steps to a partnering relationship differ for each partnership or alliance, the basic principles include:

1. Developing a mutual understanding of each party's goals and developing a written "charter", which would usually identify common goals such as safety, quality, timeliness, communication, transparency, resolution of disputes fairly, amicably, through the use of an agreed dispute resolution process, cost control and agreed levels of profitability.
2. Developing a "we" attitude in place of the customary "us versus them" attitude so that the key participants believe they can freely discuss problems and both parties will listen to and hear the other side's point of view.
3. Workshops involving key personnel from all parties with an experienced facilitator as early as possible after start up so that relationships can be fostered.
4. Regular meetings to evaluate the progress of the work and the meeting of common goals. Such evaluations are performed by key personnel within the partnering arrangement, and where appropriate the partnering "charter" can be revised.

To be successful, partnering requires a change in the mindset of all parties away from the "us and them" approach, and away from the use of the standard adversarial forms of contract. However, it should always be remembered that partnering is merely a way to facilitate good business practices, and is not a substitute for them.

The most likely way that a partnering arrangement breaks down is when the executives cease to be transparent and communicate effectively, or attempt to hide failures, mistakes and faults until the problems become so large that they become much harder to resolve without relationship breakdown. Relationship breakdown leads to legal action, which ends up as the only recourse available to resolve the issue, and of course legal action is one of the most important things that the concept of partnering is set up to avoid.

A good partnering relationship involves communication at all levels in both organizations, and early attention to any potential problems. Neither the client nor the provider of goods or services like to find out about a problematic issue near the end of a project – they tend to be much more amenable to amicable settlement or resolution of a financial or other set back when they hear about it early on rather than later in the process.

It comes back to the control of negative human traits covered in Part 1 of this book, and the promotion of the *positive* human traits which assist happy working environments rather than those which may lead to relationship breakdown.

3. Subcontractor/Vendor/Supplier Relationships

The utilization of subcontractors, vendors and suppliers can be a useful way to transfer some portion of business risk. Whilst a client is likely to require that the company it is doing business with is fully responsible for the deal it has entered into with the client, some aspects of a project can be "subcontracted" and the risk for that part of the project passed on to the subcontractor or supplier, while retaining rights of control over the subcontracted work should the subcontractor/supplier fail at any point. Conversely, if a small amount of work is being subcontracted to a company as a subcontractor on a much larger project, it would be prudent to limit the level of risk that the company undertaking the smaller amount of subcontracted work accepts. Good risk management practice would be to try and tailor the level of risk taken so that it is commensurate with the size of job being undertaken, not the size of the overall project. Even if the failure of a small supplier or subcontractor causes large losses to the main project company or client, prudent risk management would attempt to allocate these large losses appropriately. Whatever level of liability and risk is accepted by the parties in a business deal, contractual documentation should be drafted so that the level of liability and risk that each party is accepting is absolutely clear.

Eliminating Risk

Certain risks can be eliminated through contractual negotiation and documentation. Each company must assess what risks are apparent in its business dealings, but risks relating to loss or damage to persons and property, and the effects of warranties and guarantees are areas of risk which most companies must address as part of ensuring the survival of their businesses.

1. Loss/Damage to Persons and Property

When analyzing deals or business strategies where persons may get injured or killed, or physical property may get damaged, risk of loss or damage in these situations should always be covered by insurance policies that are sufficient for legal and contractual needs. The critical issue with injury/death to persons, or damage to property, is to ensure that your company's insurance program, which covers your employees and property does not end up being used by others when they have their own insurance for their employees and property.

In large ventures involving multiple entities, ranging from clients, contractors, vendors, subcontractors, third parties such as members of the public, care should be taken to ensure in the contractual documents that each entity accepts liability, howsoever caused, for its property and employees, as that entity will already hold insurance for these risks. In this way, significant areas of risk can be suitably allocated in line with existing insurance and eliminated as an area of risk from other parties. If risk is not eliminated in this way and a party accepts some level of liability for injury/death, or damage to property, of others, that liability should be limited to the level of insurance available, and preferably the proceeds of the insurance policy in case the insurance company fails to pay for any reason in the event of a claim on the policy.

This system of allocating and eliminating liability is sometimes known as a "knock for knock" arrangement, where a party accepts responsibility and liability for his employees and property, and all other parties do the same, and indemnify all other parties against loss and damage regardless of fault. In this way, a major area of potential liability and contention relating to persons and property can be removed as an issue.

Leaving the contract silent on liability in the area of persons and property is not prudent as any liability issues will be left for the courts to decide, and this may be ruinous for a company's business if the courts decide in a manner which is unfavorable and beyond the insurance and resources of that company.

The only area where liability and responsibility may sometimes be left silent in the contract is where members of the public ("third parties") are injured or property owned by members of the public ("third party property") is damaged. This tends to be left silent so that liability follows fault and the party who caused the loss or damage pays. Insurance to cover third party injury/ damage varies according the geographical location and the likely financial loss which the courts may decide on, and insurance policies should be tailored accordingly.

2. Warranties/Guarantees

It is usual for a company which is supplying products or services to provide a warranty or guarantee for the performance of the product or services. However, it is important that the provision of that warranty or guarantee is carefully defined so that the company does not commit itself to excessive financial exposure.

The general principle of a warranty or guarantee provision is:

(i) To express in writing the specific warranties or guarantees that the company supplying the product or services is providing, the timeframes under which claims may be made under the warranties and guarantees, and the remedies that may be applicable in the event that the company fails to meet the terms of the warranty or guarantee. Failure to express clearly the terms of the specific warranties or guarantees will expose the supplier/provider to whatever the position is under the law governing the contract as decided by a court or tribunal. Such an issue should never be left in doubt.

(ii) To exclude and eliminate all other warranties or guarantees that may be available expressly or by implication under the law, so that the warranties or guarantees specifically set out in the contract will be the sole and exclusive warranties which the supplier/provider is liable for. When providing a warranty or guarantee, a company should only agree to meet performance levels that are known to be within its capabilities and are tried and tested.

Everyday Business Risk:

The two everyday business issues examined above in terms of risk elimination (and most companies can identify other everyday issues that are relevant to them) show how risk can be allocated in ways which eliminate excessive financial exposure for matters which are integral to the business of many companies. Indeed such aspects of the running of a business are so basic and fundamental to the continuation of many company's business objectives that excessive risk should never be taken in such areas.

The concept is to clearly express and allocate the risks so that all parties understand where liability and responsibility reside. By clearly stating what the extent of a company's responsibility is, disputes later on are usually eliminated. These and other contractual issues will be further addressed in Chapter 12.

CHAPTER 11

POLITICAL/FOREIGN RISK AND DISPUTE RESOLUTION

In considering strategies for seeking and obtaining new business in overseas locations, it is important to recognize that certain countries and regions of the world may be less stable than your home base, but this risk may also present you with worthwhile opportunities if managed appropriately.

Political and foreign risk is generally associated with *change.* Assuming your company has assessed the operating conditions applicable to a foreign territory in which it desires to invest or undertake project work, political risk is focused on *changes* to the political system or social/economic conditions of that country from the system or conditions that existed at the time the original investment was made, or the time that the project work commenced.

All companies have key objectives, and political risk considerations centre around host country decisions that have an adverse effect on those objectives. Those decisions may relate to changes in the host country's political structure and policies, such as tax laws, tarrifs, expropriation of assets or restriction on the repatriation of profits. It could also relate to actual instability in the country from events such as riots, coups, civil war, insurrection or acts of terrorism or other increased security risks/issues for personnel, for instance kidnapping.

Minimizing political risk factors

So how can companies minimize political risk factors, either at the macro level (the level which affects all companies) or at the micro level (the level which affects only specific companies and projects).

Some guidelines are suggested below for both macro and micro level risk:

1. **Due Diligence.** Conducting research and commissioning reports from knowledgeable persons into the investment and operating issues in a country will alert the Board and its management to any potential political risk in a targeted territory. Historical facts such as how often government control changes hands, frequency of tax and regulatory changes in recent years, past record and attitudes with respect to associations with foreign parties, and general information on the culture of the country and investment climate, will help with decisions on likely risk of changes due to political issues in the foreseeable future. There are many sources for obtaining political risk ratings from specialist

analysts in the every region. Only those risks which pose a realistic threat to company performance and consequent failure to meet objectives should be considered risks needing mitigation action.

It is also a good idea to perform due diligence on potential local partners or clients such as recent litigation history of that partner or client, reputation in the territory for ethical dealing, and whether they employ family members of a senior government official or have government officials working for them in some capacity or other. If the local success of the potential partner is based on current governmental influence, then political change may see the waning of that influence with the associated consequences for the investor/ developer. Even if political change does not occur, a close eye still needs to be maintained on the ethicality of the local partner's dealings in what is a relatively unknown new business territory, as it can be counter-productive for the worldwide business of the investor to be associated with someone who may be linked to bribery or corruption.

2. **Legal System.** Does the legal system always support a government entity or does case law and precedent suggest disputes will be dealt with fairly? Is the judiciary independent of government influence?

3. **Corruption.** Does the country have a reputation for endemic corruption in concluding deals, obtaining permits, bureaucratic obstruction, and

does this corruption continue through the life of ongoing operations? There are well known sources such as the Corruption Perceptions Index and the review of internet 'blogs' on current bribery and corruption issues and practices in relation to other deals in the territory, and these can give a flavor of what to expect in a country and with potential clients. Changes of government are particularly risky where bribery and corruption is involved as changes of personnel may mean that the new government does not honor deals agreed with the previous government.

4. **Insurance.** If a decision is taken to proceed with an investment in a country which is considered a political risk, political risk insurance may be available to limit the impact of change. There are numerous insurance providers that specialize in selling political risk insurance, both at governmental level and through commercial insurance companies, with policies of insurance that would compensate a company if an adverse event occurred.

Rates for the insurance coverage depend on the country, the number of risks covered, and individual country factors, which cause rates to vary considerably from country to country. Cover often includes strikes, riots, civil commotion, terrorism, sabotage, war and civil war, and direct government action which prevents payments being made, or where currency controls or other extraordinary legislative measures reduce the value of an asset to a foreign investor. It may also cover unfair calling of bank performance bonds provided by a foreign supplier of goods or services. Political risk insurance does not cover foreign exchange or devaluation losses, which may however be covered through currency hedging specialists.

Most European governments, as well as the USA, Japan, Australia and Canada amongst others provide funding for their own national Export Credit Agencies (sometimes known as bilateral agencies or ECA's), which are designed to promote trade or other interests of that country, and support national companies which invest or carry out project development work in foreign territories. This support includes financing of exports where commercial financing is unavailable, and credit support for private sector loans made to foreign buyers to protect against the risk of non-payment by the foreign buyers/clients. The availability of ECA cover will be determined by the market limit set by the ECA for its liabilities in the country, and the creditworthiness of the client in the country. The ECA may put conditions on providing cover, such as letters of credit or payment guarantees and up-front cash payments by the client of specified portions of the contract price. The ECA will likely also require certain clauses inserted into the contract such as the right to stop work in the event of payment default. Insurance against such losses will have a financial limit specified by the ECA, with the ECA-backed company meeting a portion of the loss, often up to 10% of the loss. Availability of the cover may also be dictated by the quality of the contract conditions, particularly clauses relating to payment security, termination rights, governing law and arbitration.

In addition to ECA support of their own national companies, an agency of the World Bank, known as the Multilateral Investment Guarantee Agency (MIGA), offers protection to companies which are incorporated and have their principle place of business in a country which is a member country, or which is majority owned by nationals of a member country. Nearly 100 countries have signed the MIGA Convention and most of those have ratified the Convention. Ratification is required to participate in MIGA's programs.

It is worth remembering however that whilst some political risk insurance claims may be processed relatively quickly after small waiting periods, such as where straightforward non-payment claims, many claims can take some time, stretching into years, before any compensatory payments are made after an adverse event. This is because the exact amount of compensation is often difficult to ascertain and to agree the value of the loss. The final compensation payment may be considerably less than anticipated, may involve complex transactional issues, or may be the subject of lengthy arbitration or court proceedings.

The settlement of political risk insurance claims in

the well known case of the Dabhol Power Project in India is a case in point. This case involved Enron, GE, Bechtel, the Maharashta State Electricity Board, and Overseas Private Investment Corporation (the US Government's agency which provided investment support and political risk insurance for Enron, GE and Bechtel). The claims by Enron, GE and Bechtel took years to resolve, involved considerable expenditure of time and money, settlements were complex and involved both government-to-government arbitration and commercial arbitration as well as complex transactional issues due to the structuring of the original deal.

Political risk insurance nevertheless remains a useful, perhaps essential, tool in any investment which has been viewed by experts as high risk when the due diligence investment studies were carried out.

An alternative method for covering buyer/client payment default in foreign transactions is the use of an instrument known as a Credit Default Swap (CDS). The CDS is often used to protect against a borrower defaulting on its debt, or to speculate on the credit quality or creditworthiness of a borrower or entity. The CDS is a derivative, in other words a financial instrument whose value is based on the value of another financial instrument. CDS's are issued by banks (the sellers) and are taken out by investors (the buyers) to protect against failure of one or more of their investments.

Since the start of the 2008/09 financial crisis, the CDS as an instrument to cover default has been under pressure because of the large number of "credit events" which have occurred, but the instrument has held up well. Essentially, the buyer of the CDS makes a series of payments (premiums) to the seller of the CDS, and in the event of the underlying credit or financial instrument which is being covered by the CDS going into default (a "credit event"), the seller pays the buyer the losses covered by the CDS. A "credit event" doesn't have to be an actual payment default, it can be whatever is specified in the CDS, for instance it can be an entity going into insolvency, or even just having its credit rating downgraded.

Because CDS's are issued by banks and other major guarantors, but not by governments, there is always a potential risk that the seller will default on its coverage obligations in the event of a credit event occurring. This nearly occurred in September 2008 when AIG, the insurance corporation, required an $85 billion infusion of US Government support because it had been selling CDS protection beyond a level it could adequately cover, exposing it to potential losses in excess of $100 billion. This situation is unusual however, and the CDS market is still a huge and vital resource, estimated to be worth over $30 trillion during 2009.

The CDS was in the news again in November 2009, and the value in using CDS protection was highlighted, after a Dubai Government-owned company, Dubai World, which was considered to have good creditworthiness, requested a standstill on its debt payment obligations. This caused rises in credit default swap payments for buyers thereafter, and followed defaults and creditor write-offs in Ukrainian and Kazakhstan companies in the preceding months.

5. **Contingency Planning, Exit Strategies and Common Sense Advisory Instructions.** It is always prudent to have plans in place in the event of the occurrence of an adverse event, and also market exit strategies rather than simply reacting to an event without any prior planning having been considered. Also, many risks to personnel can be avoided by simple common sense instructions on conduct in the territory and at high risk flash points such as airports and terminals where theft and other violations can easily occur without clear safety advice.

6. **Contract Negotiations.** It would be helpful if contract terms could be negotiated which were not one-sided and inequitable where all the risk is passed from the government or public sector client in the host country to the overseas company investor/developer. Insurance cover provided for host country client default may require obtaining certain terms as stated above. Particularly when insurance is being provided, but it is prudent negotiation practice anyway, that risk should never be accepted for the following

matters: (i) insolvency of the government/public sector entity/host country client; (ii) failure of the client to pay or issue payment certificates; (iii) war, riots, civil commotion and other force majeure events; (iv) delay or inability to remit foreign exchange; (v) export/import embargoes; (vi) unfair performance bond "calling"; (vii) loss of plant/equipment due to expropriation or war/civil unrest/insurrection; (viii) inability to re-export plant/equipment at the end of a project. It is also important to consider provisions in the local laws which may override carefully negotiated terms in the contract. The governing law that will apply to the terms of a contract, and applicable dispute resolution provisions will be considered below. These can have a serious impact on the financial outcome of a project or investment.

7. **Strategic Partnering.** Mitigation of potential political risk issues can be assisted through partnering or joint venturing with a local company in the host country, or involving a local investor. This concept of local partnering is aimed at trying to prevent a loss from ever occurring, rather than the utilization of insurance to give assurance that should a loss occur, the foreign company will be compensated. Theoretically the host country should be less likely to expropriate the assets and operations of an investor/developer which is closely tied in with local participants. Utilizing local suppliers and personnel is also helpful for maintaining good relationships with the host government, and encouraging the host

government to avoid making radical political decisions.

Reducing the risk of dispute resolution

In the rush to finalize and sign a contract, executives often overlook the risk posed to the financial success of the deal by the possibility that a dispute might arise before the end of the term of the contract. Whilst no one wishes to think about a dispute arising between the parties in due course, as the relationship between the parties is likely to be amicable at the time of contract signing, it is very prudent to adequately cover the consequences of a dispute arising. It is important that one party is not badly disadvantaged should a dispute arise.

How can a party mitigate the risk of being disadvantaged in the event that a dispute arises after contract signing?

1. **Choice of Governing Law.** The choice of governing law in a contract, and the method by which disputes are resolved, may well be critical to the success of a contract overseas. The law that will govern the terms of the contract should always be stated in the contract. For preference, only those legal systems should be chosen as the governing law of the contract which are well established and have a high degree of predictability.

   The key requirement in choosing any particular legal system to govern the terms of the contract is that it upholds the terms of the deal entered into and does not arbitrarily vary the terms of the deal in the event of a dispute.

This is why systems of law such as English Law pose less of a risk to executives who have painstakingly negotiated a deal – the law will not change the deal agreed between the parties. This was emphasized in Chapter 9. The governing law of a developing nation may not give adequate protection, particularly where the laws are unsophisticated or where the judiciary are known to have limited expertise or independence.

2. **Key contractual provisions dealing with dispute resolution.** Four provisions relating to dispute resolution will dictate the success and smooth running of a dispute. The importance and suggested approach to them is addressed in this section on dispute resolution. These provisions are:

- **Forum:** In what country and in what city should the dispute resolution process take place?
- **Choice of Law:** Which country's law is to govern the contract?
- **Dispute resolution process:** The four dispute resolution processes in regular use are litigation through the law courts, arbitration utilizing tribunals, alternative dispute resolution (ADR) and expert determination.

Which is most appropriate?

- **Language:** Which language should be used in the dispute resolution process?

3. **Arbitration v Litigation.** For the critical reason of enforceability of awards (amongst many other important reasons as detailed below in this section on dispute resolution), it is generally preferable to resolve disputes through arbitration rather than litigation in developing nations or foreign territories where the law courts and legal system are unreliable.

   If there is no provision made in the contract for dispute resolution, any disputes arising out of that contract (which cannot be resolved by negotiation between the parties) are likely to have to be dealt with through litigation in the national courts of the host country.

   This could mean that the foreign company will be faced with having to resolve disputes in a foreign country under a foreign legal system in a foreign language, often with the added difficulty of having to combat corrupt practices employed in that country's legal and courts system, particularly in developing nations which do not have a good rating on the Corruption Perceptions Index.

4. **Use of Arbitration.** The way to avoid the problem of litigation in unreliable foreign courts is to include a provision in the contract for international

arbitration in the event of a dispute which cannot be amicably resolved. This will allow the parties to "pre-plan" what will happen in the event of a dispute, and they can decide in the contract they sign who will resolve their disputes, in which country/city the arbitration should take place, what law would apply to the resolution of that dispute, and which language is to be used for the purpose of the dispute hearing.

Arbitration is usually a quicker and cheaper means of resolving disputes than national courts, even in developed nations with sophisticated legal systems, and is certainly more private, as the proceedings, paperwork and judgments are generally not made public.

Where disputes arise over work being undertaken in developing nations, it is usually preferable to insist on arbitration under established rules in a third country venue where good arbitrators are readily available. Some of the most commonly used forums for international disputes which are well respected around the world are (a) UNCITRAL (United Nations Commission on International Trade Law) Arbitration Rules administered from The Hague, Netherlands; (b) International Chamber of Commerce (ICC) Rules administered from Paris and Geneva; (c) The London Court of International Arbitration, administered from London, England; (d) The Stockholm Chamber of Commerce Rules; and (d) for disputes in Asia, the Hong Kong International Arbitration Centre Rules or the Singapore International Arbitration

Centre Rules are both well respected. It is always worth using arbitration centers that have good reputations due the high quality panels of arbitrators available and where little debate will ensue between the negotiating parties to a contractual deal about these sets of arbitration rules due to their reputation for reasoned awards and their accessible locations.

5. **Arbitration and the New York Convention of 1958.** It is important to ensure that any judgment obtained is enforceable in the host country. The New York Convention of 1958 is a multilateral international convention on the recognition and enforcement of foreign arbitral awards, which has been signed by 144 countries (as at June 2010), and requires courts of any country which is a signatory of the Convention to enforce arbitral awards. This makes the assets of a party which are based in the host country much easier to access after an arbitral award. Winning disputes, with all the time and expense involved, is no use if the final award cannot be enforced. This is why arbitration in international disputes is far preferable to litigation in national courts, particularly in developing nations. To ensure that the country you are negotiating a deal in is a signatory to the New York Convention, it is worth checking the status of signatory countries who have ratified the 1958 Convention on the Enforcement of Foreign Arbitral Awards on the UNCITRAL website. Perhaps more importantly, it is worth checking the countries that have *not* signed

up to the enforcement of foreign arbitration awards. There are 51 of these countries as of June 2010 and they include places where large deals are often done, particularly in the oil sector.

6. **Alternative Dispute Resolution and Expert Determination.** To save time and money, and hopefully to assist the process of the parties remaining amicable, technical disputes are often best resolved through expert determination by a specialist in the technical field rather than by lawyers. Similarly, the use of mediation as a way of bringing the parties round a table to discuss their differences with the assistance of a mediator/facilitator often resolves disputes at little cost and saves the very damaging process of formal arbitration or court proceedings. It is remarkable how often disputes arise through lack of communication between the parties about the issues of one or other of the parties, and simply bringing the parties together before an independent third party is all that is needed to resolve the issues.

7. **Risk allocation in Contracts.** Where parties have fairly allocated risks, disputes may be less likely to arise. This is because the interests of the parties are often best served by allocating risks to the party best able to control or handle them, rather than passing risk to the weakest party because this is easy to do. Proper allocation of risks during contract negotiation can prevent claims and performance difficulties later on, which

cause all parties to suffer impacts on objectives such as profit, cost control, quality and on-time completion.

8. **Conduct of the parties during dispute settlement.** Before the parties to a dispute end up in court or arbitration, they will usually have met one or more times to try and discuss a settlement of their grievances. As with the conduct of executives at the time they negotiated the deal, the key attributes of which were extensively discussed in Chapter 5 ("How to negotiate to reduce risk"), the conduct of executives at any meeting to discuss settlement of disputes should be addressed in the same way.

The same principles such as preparation, the ability to listen and observe, understanding manners and customs, and the ability to be patient and courteous even when you may feel frustrated with progress are all invaluable attributes.

Successful negotiation of settlements is about the ability to focus on a reasonable remedy. It is not about airing your grievances in a destructive manner. What is past is past, and a reasonable approach to the search for a remedy which can satisfy both parties is paramount. It is certainly a good time to be realistic, and concede ground on overly optimistic claims, or overly defensive attitudes.

If resolution of the dispute cannot be achieved

through reasonable conduct, you will always have your "day in court" where all grievances will be fully documented and aired, at great expense, but the purpose of a pre-legal action meeting is to explore whether there is the opportunity for a fair settlement. Pointing out fault, using provocative language ("it's your fault", "you must be joking", "be honest", "are you kidding") and so forth is not going to help matters. Listen carefully, question carefully, and by discovering what the other side's true needs are may be enlightening in the search for a settlement. It may be useful, for instance, to look at previous solutions achieved, use mutually acceptable third party standards or sources to measure success or failure where appropriate, or previous precedents in other similar cases.

Focus on the key attributes of successful negotiation: to observe, to be patient and to listen. Much can be achieved this way.

CHAPTER 12

SPECIAL RISK CONSIDERATIONS FOR CONTRACTORS, SUPPLIERS, AND SERVICE PROVIDERS; NOTES FOR DEVELOPERS/BUYERS

The Attitude/Approach of the Developer/Buyer is critical

The problem with the development of projects and systems that are often large and complex is that it is not unusual for them to proceed despite a high degree of uncertainty. Often at the time initial financial commitments are made, factors ranging from the design, scope of works, the period for completion, and the likely final cost can be uncertain. As will be seen, buyer's benefit from reducing uncertainty.

With all these potential uncertainties, it would seem prudent that the developers, financiers, and owners/ buyers make a careful review of risks that the project could face. Such a review should allow them to consider how these risks could be allocated most appropriately to ensure that their objectives are met. Key objectives would normally include a timeframe for completion, and a target price/budget.

The project has the best chance of being completed within a reasonable projected timeframe and price, with the minimum number of disputes and disruptions as are reasonably possible along the way, if a realistic allocation of the key risks is undertaken. Sensible risk analysis and allocation will reduce uncertainty. Reduction of uncertainty increases the chances of project success.

The attitude of the developer/owner/buyer ("the buyer") will be critical in the early stages of project developments. The buyer will normally have been planning a project for a lengthy period with his own advisors before he reaches the point where he has produced a document which sets out how he envisages his project being developed, and how the roles, responsibilities and risks should be structured as between the parties.

Many of his ideas about risk allocation will therefore be formulated long before the contractor/supplier/service provider ("the contractor") has the chance to price the buyer's document, often called an "invitation to bid" document, and has the chance to comment on the document's allocation of risks.

Amending a risk allocation structure already embedded into a buyer's document against which various competitors are pricing may therefore be difficult and limited, so the approach of the buyer in the bid documents he produces is critical to how a project is likely to be priced and how it develops over the project development period.

Risk Spectrum

The buyer's approach can cover a vast spectrum of ways to allocate risk. Each way will produce a different consequence. The consequences may involve, for better or worse, an impact on pricing, quality or safety, time schedules, or the level or extent of disputes and adversarial conduct by the contractor.

At one end of the spectrum there is the position of the buyer who drafts the bid documents in such a way that requires the contractor to accept the entire risk inherent in performance of the contractor's work scope for an agreed price. In this way he can report back to his fellow investors or shareholders that the contractor is locked in and that any problem that arises for that moment on is at the risk of the contractor.

This position has theoretical appeal, but it creates an adversarial approach from project commencement, and when problems do arise, it would be unusual to find matters resolved without dispute resolution being required, and without price and time being affected. Techniques used by both parties in these situations will be discussed shortly, but depending on how various matters were structured at the time the deal was finalized, the buyer may not be the clear winner that he expects to be.

At the other end of the spectrum, some buyers have concluded that it is more cost effective to enter into well structured deals where risk is allocated in a more sophisticated manner, particularly in large complex developments, with the utilization of non-standard documentation tailored to the specific deal, as for instance happens regularly in the oil and gas, and petro chemical industries. These buyers tend to find that they have fewer delays and disputes, a better end product/facility, and bids that are more realistically priced with less excessive contingency pricing because the risks have not been allocated in an unbalanced manner.

Buyer realism

What is a buyer's primary objective in awarding work to a contractor?

Is it a fixed price (which may also be a high price) but with the allocation of the greatest possible risk placed with the contractor and priced into the deal, which may help to minimize the impact of cost and time overruns? Or is it a potentially lower price, which may be a fixed price but may possibly be based on other pricing criteria, with risk being allocated in a different manner, which may ensure less chance of failure by a contractor before the end of the project?

Project difficulties can arise where the following risk allocation principles are significantly varied:

- Risk should be borne by the party best able to control or manage the risk.
- Risk should be borne by the party best able to foresee the risk.
- Risk should be borne by the party best able financially to bear the risk.
- Risk which is unquantifiable should not be borne by a party with limited assets.

A buyer can increase the chances of project success by:

- Evaluating the risks relating to a project himself before issuing bid documents to a contractor.
- Having evaluated the risks himself, passing on to the contractor as much relevant information on

the project as possible to enable the contractor to make his own assessment/evaluation of the risks identified at the time the contractor undertakes the pricing of the project, rather than leaving it to the contractor to guess at the risks he may encounter and possibly 'gamble' with pricing risk.

- Where the buyer has evaluated the various potential project risks, use the contract documents to allocate the risks between the parties in accordance with the risk allocation principles set out above.
- Choose a contractor that has suitable and known experience in the work to be undertaken, has a sound financial standing at the time of the bid, and has acceptable quality and safety standards. Any compromise on experience, financial status, quality or safety in pursuit of a low price has a far greater chance of leading to project difficulties in due course, and the possibility of failure by the buyer to achieve his objective of a successfully project completed on time, in budget, with performance and quality standards accomplished, and with the minimum of disputes.
- Be realistic about the timeframe/program for completion of the project and revenue commencement. Delay in completion can be the greatest cause of extra cost, and of loss of financial return on investment.

It can never be said too many times: Buyer's benefit from reducing uncertainty. Buyers want the best working plant, facility or development possible. They want the facility to meet its performance specifications, and they want to make the money from the facility that they projected at the time they decided to invest in the facility. It is little use therefore to a buyer to find that the contractor collapses in financial, known-how or resource difficulties before a project is complete because the balance of risk had been hopelessly misallocated or because the choice of a "cheap" contractor, which pleased the Board at the time the contract was signed, has now unraveled. In the construction industry, the many standard contract forms can assist the parties to allocate risk in a balanced manner, and these documents are a good starting point for many construction developments.

Catastrophic risk, which if it came to pass would cause a contractor to become insolvent, should not be allocated to a contractor, and a contractor should not accept, or be forced to accept, this sort of risk. Buyer's need to retain their sense of realism, and remember that a well-executed project will produce revenues over the life of the facility, and (whilst it would be nice if it never happened) cost overruns can be amortized by the buyer over the life of the facility, whereas the contractor receives no further revenue after the project has been completed. This has been referred to as the "whole life" concept of risk sharing on a project.

Contractor self-preservation methods

There are certain rules which help a contractor to avoid putting his business at risk. It should always be remembered that few businesses stay in business long if they make losses on deals they enter into. This concept has been addressed in Chapter 8 as part of consideration of risk principles. It is worthy of further comment here: ten key issues that a contractor should always be sure he has covered.

1. Never accept a "take it or leave it" approach by the buyer.

A smart buyer will try and find himself in the position of being a beneficiary of a price war between contractors competing for his business deal. Contractors should be aware of situations where this objective is being attempted by a buyer. How can a contractor discover whether a buyer is attempting to create a price war? The best indication of this is by considering the number of bidders that the buyer is allowing to become involved in bidding for a project.

It is not unusual for buyers to adopt 'price reduction' tactics during the bidding phase of a project, (and even during the execution phase), which are designed to reduce the cost of the project to the buyer at the expense of the winning contractor's profit margin. This tactic should be identified by the contractor as early as possible and steps taken to combat it.

Where an excessive number of bidders are allowed to bid for the work, say, in excess of four bidders, and the bid list consists of a number of contractors who are fierce competitors, then the likelihood is that a price war will ensue which will end up reducing the profit margin on the work to a small, or non-existent, level without any commensurate reduction in risk associated with the work.

Also, the buyer will be able to adopt a "take it or leave it" attitude to contract terms: if you don't accept the risk, some other contractor will. Business development managers of contractors love to hear (and report back to their bosses) that their company is 'favored' by the buyer – this type of statement should be treated with great care, as it may well be designed to soften up a contractor into accepting greater risk at a lower price on the basis of accepting a deal quickly. Sometimes the contractor may accept riskier conditions, and reduced margins than he would normally concede, then find the deal fails to materialize as quickly as expected after having already given away more than is safe. He then finds that a further cut in price may still be required to fight off competition from others who have been "made aware" of his company's position.

2. Know the Bottom Line

The answer to price war tactics by a buyer is for a contractor to always know what his 'bottom line' is in relation to the balance of risk and reward. Sophisticated negotiating requires the contractor to clearly specify his desired contractual position in relation to the price he is prepared to carry out the work for, at the time he submits his bid.

However, if stating his detailed analysis of the buyer's proposed contract terms will reduce his chances of getting to the negotiating table (and getting to the negotiating table must be the goal of any bidder, so he can assess the true standpoint/attitude of the buyer), then his bid must be sufficiently qualified so that he cannot be considered by the buyer to have accepted as part of his bid an unquantifiable risk, or a risk that has not been properly priced in his bid. This may require the bidder to condition his bid language in very sophisticated terms initially, particularly where the bid may also require a 'good faith' bid bond issued by a bank to be submitted with the bid.

Going beyond the 'bottom line' to obtain an award only leads to one place: losses. Losses lead to failure. A contractor should always retain the ability to say "no" should a deal move to a point where the bottom line has been exceeded and losses can be anticipated if the deal was signed on those proposed terms. This inevitably leads to project difficulties, a constant battle to stem the level of losses, and the inevitable disputes as the project reaches its conclusion. Ensuring a deal is not accepted which has gone beyond the "bottom line", is the part of the effective use of company checks and balances that was discussed earlier in the book – no one person should be able to overrule an analysis that forecasts losses if the deal is accepted.

3. **Monitor carefully buyer requests and decision-making after award.**

Once the contractor has received the project award and has commenced execution of the work, he should carefully consider how the buyer acts when decisions need to be made. The contractor needs to understand clearly who makes the buyer's decisions, and who it is that merely administers decisions and has little or no decision-making authority. Failure to understand this may cost the contractor money and lead to disputes.

The critical decisions made by the buyer's executives after contract award are issues relating to (a) progress payments and (b) payment for work that the contractor is asked to do which is outside the original scope of work covered by the contract award.

The ability of a contractor to control its actions and cash flow relating to buyer requests after award will depend on the terms of contract it negotiated pre-award. It is imperative in negotiating the terms of the contract that those contract terms do *not* require the contractor to carry out any work or buy any goods which are outside the original scope of work before the price for that extra work or any additional materials have been agreed in writing.

Clauses in contracts relating to requests or instructions to carry out additional work or make additional purchases are often overlooked in the contract negotiations. After the project work is underway, the buyer makes additional requests and the contractor discovers that he would be in breach of contract for failing to act on the instructions of a buyer to carry out additional services or purchase further materials, even before the price and terms for those additional goods and services have been agreed. Not only could failure to adequately cover this issue in the contract affect the contractor's credit lines and cash flow, but it may result in disputes over the value of the extra work or goods in due course.

Buyers know that most contractors are schedule-driven, because the financial damages that arise for failure to complete the project on time are often significant, and the longer a contractor is on site or using resources on a project the more it costs him. Contractors can therefore be anticipated by buyers to undertake additional work requests/instructions first, to try and maintain schedule as far as possible, in the anticipation of a "fair" response from the buyer.

However, unless the contractor has negotiated a good clause in his contract on when he is required to commence the undertaking of additional work, commencing work without a written agreement on time and pricing issues for the additional work leaves the contractor in a position where the negotiating strength is in the hands of the buyer. The buyer can simply delay agreement on the terms of the additional work until the contractor accepts a discounted price or reduced profit margin for the extra work undertaken. The contractor is often then using key resources at a far too low return on investment, to the benefit of the buyer but considerable detriment of the contractor.

The contractor should also try and avoid allowing the buyer to settle the payment of small additional work orders whilst leaving "open" a large value additional work order (sometimes known as a "change order"). Buyers often require extra time to review the terms and pricing of large additional work orders, but this should not be done at the expense of the contractor's cash flow and credit lines.

The best policy of a contractor is not to commence work on large value change orders before agreement has been reached in writing with the buyer over the payment terms, time extensions for project completion, and the actual price of the additional work. This necessitates getting the contract terms right before signing.

4. Pay attention to record-keeping.

Wherever a dispute arises over a matter in a contract, the one issue which will make the difference about what you are paid in the end is the standard of your record-keeping. This subject will be addressed in more detail shortly in discussing in greater depth the subject of claims and change orders, but contractors must keep good records to combat buyers who hold back monies which a contractor considers is owed to him. Good record keeping will help a contractor to decide whether to settle quickly with a buyer to avert a potential cash flow shortage, or pursue a contractual dispute process. A contractor will be in a far better position to decide what to do if he has kept good records. Without good records he risks his case being rejected by a court or tribunal for lack of adequate detail should the matter progress that far, quite apart from the time and money he will spend pursuing the matter (and the buyer is unlikely to assist the contractor's cash flow once a matter is in dispute).

5. Specify clearly the conditions applicable to Bank Bonds and Performance Guarantees

In the event that a contractor agrees to provide a buyer with bank bonding or performance guarantees (or both) to assure the buyer that the contractor will perform his obligations, the contractor should nevertheless ensure that the terms for the provision of these documents are clearly specified.

Bank bonding requires trust that the buyer will not unfairly "make a call" on the bonding and request the bank to make a payment without a sound basis for such bank payment. The contract, and the terms on the bond itself, should therefore specify clearly the basis on which payment from a bank can be made, failing which the contractor could face both a cash flow shortage and a lengthy contractual dispute to recover his money.

Similarly, where a contractor is required to provide a performance-related guarantee, for instance that a plant or facility will meet a stated through-put capacity, product yields, product components manufactured and so forth, care must be taken in the drafting of the performance obligation of the contractor that the buyer has also met his input requirements before the contractor can be held liable for performance failure.

The performance guarantee should also exclude liability on the part of the contractor for failure of the plant or facility to meet the performance requirements resulting from ordinary wear and tear, corrosion, erosion, improper maintenance, or improper operation of the plant, or failure to follow manuals or supplier advisory notes.

6. **Exclude liability for economic or consequential loss**

Any liability which could put a company's entire business at risk should never be accepted in a contract. Certain liabilities therefore need to be specifically excluded. These are liabilities which are unquantifiable. Each contractual deal has its own potential liabilities which can cause the entire business to be at risk if such a liability came to pass, and any liability of this sort should be listed and excluded. These risks come into a generic category called "economic" or "consequential" loss, but each deal needs to specify these liabilities specifically, such as loss of revenues, loss of profit, loss of product, or loss of production. It is irrelevant whether such losses arise directly or indirectly out of the services provided to a buyer. They must be excluded. Often contractors simply exclude liability for "indirect or consequential" losses, but these words are not only unclear, but certainly do not exclude anything which arises *directly* out of the services provided by the contractor.

The law has been clear on this issue for some time. Time after time clauses have come before the courts using language such as the following language from a landmark case over thirty years ago: *"we are not under any circumstances to be liable for any consequential loss or damage caused or arising by reason of late supply or fault, failure, or defect in any material or goods supplied by us or by reason of the same not being of the quality or specification ordered or by any other matter whatsoever".* This language looks on the face of it to be fairly thorough, enabling the seller to exclude matters such as loss of profit or revenue, but on analysis it fails to exclude any liability which arises *directly* out of the goods or services provided. The courts held in that case that those words did not exclude any liability which arose "directly and naturally in the ordinary course of events".

A contractor must therefore *specifically* exclude any liability which could put the business of the contractor at risk if the liability arises. To confirm the importance of this contractual position, after a methanol converter exploded in India severely damaging a plant and causing all production to cease in 1992, the plant owner sued the contractor for its loss of profit, which would have caused the likely insolvency or liquidation of the contractor's business if the owner had been successful.

Fortunately, the contractor had been wise enough in the contractual terms signed by the parties to state that *"in no event did the contractor accept any liability by reason of its performance or obligation under this contract for loss of anticipated profits, catalyst, raw material and products"*. The clause was lengthy and contained a lot of other language relating to consequential loss and other matters, but the key words were that the contractor had specifically excluded liability for the very matter which he was sued for, which was loss of anticipated profits. Even though the plant may have failed to perform within its design parameters, the insertion of this contractual language saved the company from financial disaster.

If a party is entering into a contract in a territory and under a law which may be unclear on liability issues, it is best at minimum to make the contractual position clear. That way at least the courts understand what the intentions of the parties were at the time they signed the contract. Do not leave the contract silent on a matter which could put a company's entire business at risk if that matter came to pass, such as the issues noted above. Such liabilities should preferably always be clearly excluded, or at minimum clearly limited to a level which would not put the company's future at risk. However, because unclear laws can severely damage a company if risks such as this come to pass and the company gets involved in litigation anyway, even when the contract contains clear language, it is preferable to use laws which are predictable, and tried and tested.

From a buyer's point of view, whilst it is not in its interests to see a company who it is doing business with fail, because no one obtains financial benefit that way, it may be wise to attempt to find a middle ground on such an issue, such as the contractor taking some level of liability which is limited, and which can perhaps be covered by insurance. Sharing risk benefits both parties, and covers the key risk principles that the risk should be borne by the party best able to control, manage, or financially bear the risk.

7. Be clear about what liability is accepted for delays to a project

Delays on a project tend to cause disputes. Delays cost money and unless a contractor has set out clearly in the contract what his rights and liabilities are in the event of delays occurring, that contractor is likely to lose money. When executives sign contracts for project developments, before they sign, they should always be clear about what will happen in the event of a delay to the agreed completion date for the project.

When a contractor is negotiating a contract, it would be a reasonable principle to try and negotiate a fair deal. It is much easier to negotiate from a position of fairness than to try and negotiate a clause which benefits one party more than another and unbalances the risk/reward ratio and the risk principles stated above that risk should be borne by the party best able to control and manage the risk, or financially bear the risk.

It is difficult therefore for parties who are negotiating over the terms of what will happen in the event of a delay to argue against a proposal that is reasonable. In the case of delays, a fair position is that the contractor should accept responsibility for delays to a project that are *within his control*, and should not expect time extensions to the contractual completion date or payment for additional costs incurred in these circumstances. The contractor should not however accept responsibility for delays *outside his control,* and should be entitled to extensions of time to the contractual completion date and payment for his prolongation costs in these circumstances, *except* in the case of force majeure (being an event beyond the control of both parties) when he should merely be entitled to an extension of time to the contractual completion date that equates to the period of delay.

It is usual for a buyer to require a contractor to complete his defined work scope by a specific date, and if the contractor fails to meet that date the contractor would be in breach of contract, and the buyer would be entitled to various remedies for such breach by the contractor. Where delays to the start up of a plant, facility or development cause a buyer to lose revenue, a contractor could have significant liability, which could put his solvency at risk in serious cases of delay where a buyer's loss of revenue is significant.

It is usual therefore for a contractor to limit his

liability for delay to a specific figure per day, week or other period, with a maximum liability for delay. This liability is sometimes known as 'liquidated damages' or a 'penalty', depending on the jurisdiction of the contract. The language used is important, because what is enforceable varies from jurisdiction to jurisdiction. Sometimes the phrase "penalty" is enforceable for delay liability, and sometimes "liquidated damages". Liquidated damages should always be expressed as a genuine pre-estimate of the likely losses applicable in the event of delay.

What is important is for the liability for delay to be *clearly stated* so that before the contract commences the parties know what will happen in the event of delay where fault is attributable to the contractor.

Where a buyer has caused the contractor to be delayed, the contract should contain a clear entitlement to an extension of time to the completion date for such delay, and payment of the contractor's extra costs incurred relating to the delay period. Often buyers simply state that they "may" award extra costs or that they "have the power to award" extra costs. This is not a clear entitlement and should not be accepted by the contractor as it may cost him dearly later on should the buyer delay the completion date.

The contractor will of course have to prove that he is entitled to extra costs and an extension of time to complete, and therefore, as stated earlier, he must keep careful records. Many delay claims by contractors fail because they did not follow the requirements of the contract or failed to justify the extra time or costs through lack of adequate records. For instance, if the contract requires the contractor to give notice of a delay or extra costs within a particular timeframe in order to obtain extra time or costs, then he should strictly adhere to this requirement.

It is therefore imperative that all parties understand what the contract says, and follow those terms carefully. This way, the likelihood of disputes and difficulties arising later are significantly reduced. Arguments over entitlements are normally a result of lack of records for the delay or costs claimed.

Delay is a serious risk to the cash flow and potential livelihood of a contractor, who has no ability after completion of the project to amortize those extra costs over a lengthy subsequent period of revenue generation unlike the buyer. He must therefore know his rights in the event of delay occurring, follow the terms of the contract precisely, and keep meticulous records related to the delay and costs he wishes to obtain relief for.

8. Be clear about what documents are required to complete a project

In the rush to sign a contract, contractors often do not carefully consider the documents that will be required by the buyer to allow the buyer to give the contractor a certificate to show that the project is complete. This should be made absolutely clear in the contract, otherwise the contractor could find himself in delay purely because the buyer is making unreasonable requests as to what he requires to bring the contractor's work to a close. As mentioned above, delay is costly, and it would be negligent for a contractor to find himself in delay caused simply through documentation or administrative requirements of the buyer.

9. Define clearly the scope of work

It is imperative that the scope of work to be performed by the contractor is clearly defined. If this has not occurred, there may be arguments later on during the performance of the work when a buyer considers that some portion of work should be done within the existing contract price rather than as additional work. This could be very costly for the contractor.

The scope of work document should only contain a description of the work, and should not detail any other matters, particularly contractual matters, as this may unwittingly conflict with the terms of contract that the parties have painstakingly negotiated. The contract should always take precedent over all other documents.

10. Cash flow, currency, and material pricing fluctuations

The quickest way to default on contractual obligations and responsibilities and put a project at risk is when the contractor is struggling with liquidity issues. Cash liquidity is fundamental to survival.

The following points should be well known to the

treasury departments of contractors, but are worth briefly repeating here:

(a) Advance payments. A sufficient advance payment or payments from the Client to enable the contractor to stay ahead of all financial obligations is vital. Contractors are not financiers, and business development executives should always remember this. Consequently, positive cash flow is a pre-requisite in negotiating payment terms.

(b) Currency. Currency hedging is critical when contracts are priced in more than one currency. Or where materials, components and the like are being purchased in a currency other than the one in which you are being paid by the Client. Hedging is a vital method of transferring pricing risk, and will be well known to treasury departments.

(c) Price fluctuation of materials. The probability of major pricing fluctuations of metals and other key project materials over relatively short periods of time has become a major risk in the current market. If a contractor is executing long term contracts in which materials such as steel or cement need to be purchased, and the contract entered into has a fixed price, the risk of major pricing fluctuation of such materials cannot be taken by a contractor. The contractor must therefore agree a long term deal for pricing stability with the materials supplier, which may be difficult, or exclude this element from the fixed price arrangements with the Client.

The Foreseeability Test and Soils/Ground Conditions

One of the riskiest areas in construction work is the ground conditions encountered by the contractor. The discovery of ground conditions that are different from those that the parties expected to find is likely to be costly and have a significant effect on the project schedule.

The risk is so significant in terms of the impact on profitability for a contractor, and possibly even viability of a project for the owner, that the manner in which this risk is handled is vital.

The problem comes down to how the issue has been dealt with in the contract terms negotiated by the parties. Executives will find it well worth their while taking the time necessary to negotiate the terms of this clause carefully and understand clearly what has been agreed. Risk allocation can range from an owner passing all risk to the contractor at one extreme to a more balanced allocation between the parties at the other end of the spectrum. The range of technical and commercial deals that parties reach is vast.

The significance of this risk was acknowledged during the 1970's by many of the leading construction institutions around the world, and one of the most widely used sets of contract conditions (FIDIC) in the international market introduced a method for dealing with the risk. FIDIC (Federation Internationale des Ingenieurs-Conseils) and also the UK's Institution of Civil Engineers (ICE) introduced a "foreseeability test". This test approached the risk on the basis that the contractor should only price for those risks which an experienced contractor could reasonably be expected to foresee at the time of bid.

This test meant that owners had to properly plan and investigate site conditions before inviting contractors to bid for the construction work, and inhibited owners from simply passing the risk on to contractors and taking no responsibility for site data provided. It also reduced the size of price contingencies that contractors added to their contract price.

Many government contract terms contain some form of "changed site conditions" clause, but the terms vary from deal to deal and country to country. Private developers often approach the risk initially in the bid documents by passing as much risk on to the contractor as possible. Whatever position is proposed by an owner at the start of a negotiation, there is usually significant discussion before the issue is concluded in the contract document.

Essentially, the issue revolves around the encountering by a contractor of physical site conditions that differ materially from the conditions that he should have reasonably expected to find at the time he entered into the deal. This could be because the site information provided by the owner proves to be incorrect, or it could be a condition which no one could have reasonably anticipated, such as the discovery of artificial debris.

Contractors are certainly advised to include a "changed conditions" clause into their contracts, which grants the contractor suitable cost and schedule relief, as the general position under common law is that a contractor assumes the risk of increased direct or indirect costs as well as impact costs such as an extended schedule from unforeseen site conditions unless the contractor's performance is rendered impossible by the acts or omissions of another party, or by law or act of god.

A typical provision introduced into a contract by an owner might shift the risk to the contractor by placing on him the duty to investigate and assume responsibility for verifying site conditions and shortcomings in the specifications, and disclaiming liability for any information provided. Contractors should insist on being able to rely on data provided by the owner so there is a base line position in the event that site conditions change.

How the final deal on risk allocation for changed ground conditions is worked out varies considerably from deal to deal, but risk can be mitigated by the following suggestions:

- Ensure that data provided by the owner can be relied on;
- Limit the liability for the cost of changed conditions in the contract;
- Limit the liability for an increased schedule due to changed conditions in the contract;
- Include cost and schedule contingencies;
- Obtain insurance coverage where available for specific risks;
- Conduct additional soil investigations either before or after award allowing the risk allocation to be reviewed after receipt of the additional information;

- Ensure the contract includes a clear entitlement to claim additional costs and schedule extension if the contractor can show that the conditions have changed;

This issue is extremely complex, so clearly stating in the contract as to what the position is in the event that changed conditions are encountered is essential. This is not a matter which can be left to chance.

Contractors: The Final Word

All businesses must pay attention to the risks they take on as part of their everyday business. Contractors however operate in a particularly risky environment where uncertainty is a key feature of their work and there is only one time to make profits – before their work or services have been completed. There isn't a constant stream of revenue, like owners of facilities, plants and developments have, against which losses can be amortized, and their asset base is usually small. It therefore takes only small lapses in discipline relating to risk assessment and contract negotiation to adversely affect the future prospects of a company.

Contractors should be particularly vigilant therefore to ensure that they do not fall into any of the following traps which can bring about the failure of their company:

- Too much change at one time in the way a company operates: introduction of new services, new systems, new clients, new markets, sudden increases in business and entry into new territories not previously encountered have long been acknowledged as sources of risk. Before allowing any of these circumstances to arise, a full risk assessment as to the company's suitability to undertake this new work should be carried out. Executives should be realistic about the company's ability to perform in these new areas of activity.

- Too little change when changing circumstances demand a different approach: when a company relies too heavily on its core business activity and core personnel when the market and demands are changing, eventually it will fail. Many contractors changed too slowly when times were good and then entered new markets without the skills, know-how and resources that were required, and which could have been acquired at the right time. Executives missed those acquisition and development opportunities when the time was right, leading to slow decline and ultimately failure or acquisition by others.

- Key executive ego needs carefully managing: in-built checks and balances must never be overridden. Senior managers should never be allowed to "do their own thing" uncontrolled. Deals should always be accepted on the right terms. No deal should be taken which contains terms which could put the company at risk if the worst case scenario occurred. Executives should always remember that understanding the potential losses and mitigating them produces profit – it is not how much a company can make on a deal, it is always about understanding how much a company can lose that brings success.

PART 3

CONCLUSION

CHAPTER 13

CONCLUSION

With all that can go wrong, it's a wonder that there are so many success stories. What makes one company successful and another fail? It comes down to the way *people* conduct the business of the company.

It is rare for a company to be floored by any one event. It is far more likely that the decisions that are made by the managers of that company over lengthy periods of time will cause that company to fail.

By following the simple rules for managing risk set out in this book, the prospect for success of the business will increase substantially.

The problem is that human frailties constantly get in the way. Just when success is looming on the horizon, we knock it down with the multitude of negative human traits we possess, such as worry, fear, hubris, greed, selfishness, anger, and of course ego. Then when failure arrives, we like to blame it on external factors, but it is our conduct when times were good, and the way we react to the difficulties when they arrive, that makes the difference between survival or demise, success or failure.

We should try and create an environment where success is bred, through awareness of others, through our attitude and through good communication. Unhappiness does not create satisfaction or a good working environment. Attitudes must change. It goes as deep as our attitude towards capitalism itself. This is because the underlying logic of capitalism values short-term profit and perpetual growth above all else. A longer term view is required, and a changed attitude towards those around us.

There should be no significant difference in the way your corporate and private lives are conducted. Easy-to-follow rules for better conduct of your business and your life can never be stated too many times. Here they are again:

- **Be aware of those around you**. It is good for business and good for your personal life. Develop the ability to listen, to observe, and to be patient. These attributes, if performed diligently, will tell you more than you are likely to need to be successful. You will learn and understand very quickly. Your knowledge will be the basis for your success.

- **Pay attention to your image**. Consider how other people view your presence. Do you dress well, do you smile, are you relaxed, do you use your eyes, are you fit and healthy? If you are the "face" of your company in any capacity, impression is vital.

- **Be disciplined**. Preparation for everything you do cannot be overlooked. Failure to prepare adequately for meetings, failure to produce well-researched notes, because of lack of time is unacceptable. Good decisions require an uncluttered mind, so remove the clutter from around you. Keep a clear mind and don't waste time on unimportant and meaningless things. With clarity of mind, worry and fear are diminished.

- **Keep things simple**. Try and look at the big picture. The more complicated a matter becomes, the more the detail drags you down, the less likely you are to find the best solution. If you do only one thing in a day, make sure it's the most important thing.

It is the combination of good control of the risks that are caused by people, and good control and management of commercial risks that brings success. This is the perfect interaction of people and events. By understanding and putting into practice the principles that have been outlined in this book, businesses can be transformed and long term success achieved. As each business changes its ways, as people change, commerce and industry as a whole can be transformed.

Finally, and above all, keep in the back of your mind that one day you will move on from the company you work for, or retire. Make sure you can say that the company you worked for is a better place for your efforts, because you were around.

APPENDIX 1

TRANSPARENCY INTERNATIONAL
2009 CORRUPTION PERCEPTIONS INDEX

- The Corruption Perceptions Index (CPI) table shows a country's ranking and score, the number of surveys used to determine the score, and the confidence range of the scoring.

- The rank shows how one country compares to others included in the index. The CPI score indicates the perceived level of public-sector corruption in a country/territory.

- The CPI is based on 13 independent surveys. However, not all surveys include all countries. The surveys used column indicates how many surveys were relied upon to determine the score for that country.

- The confidence range indicates the reliability of the CPI scores and tells us that allowing for a margin of error, we can be 90% confident that the true score for this country lies within this range.

Rank	Country/Territory	CPI 2009 Score	Surveys Used	Confidence Range
1	New Zealand	9.4	6	9.1 - 9.5
2	Denmark	9.3	6	9.1 - 9.5
3	Singapore	9.2	9	9.0 - 9.4
3	Sweden	9.2	6	9.0 - 9.3
5	Switzerland	9.0	6	8.9 - 9.1
6	Finland	8.9	6	8.4 - 9.4
6	Netherlands	8.9	6	8.7 - 9.0
8	Australia	8.7	8	8.3 - 9.0
8	Canada	8.7	6	8.5 - 9.0
8	Iceland	8.7	4	7.5 - 9.4
11	Norway	8.6	6	8.2 - 9.1
12	Hong Kong	8.2	8	7.9 - 8.5
12	Luxembourg	8.2	6	7.6 - 8.8
14	Germany	8.0	6	7.7 - 8.3
14	Ireland	8.0	6	7.8 - 8.4
16	Austria	7.9	6	7.4 - 8.3
17	Japan	7.7	8	7.4 - 8.0
17	United Kingdom	7.7	6	7.3 - 8.2
19	United States	7.5	8	6.9 - 8.0

Rank	Country/Territory	CPI 2009 Score	Surveys Used	Confidence Range
20	Barbados	7.4	4	6.6 - 8.2
21	Belgium	7.1	6	6.9 - 7.3
22	Qatar	7.0	6	5.8 - 8.1
22	Saint Lucia	7.0	3	6.7 - 7.5
24	France	6.9	6	6.5 - 7.3
25	Chile	6.7	7	6.5 - 6.9
25	Uruguay	6.7	5	6.4 - 7.1
27	Cyprus	6.6	4	6.1 - 7.1
27	Estonia	6.6	8	6.1 - 6.9
27	Slovenia	6.6	8	6.3 - 6.9
30	United Arab Emirates	6.5	5	5.5 - 7.5
31	Saint Vincent and the Grenadines	6.4	3	4.9 - 7.5
32	Israel	6.1	6	5.4 - 6.7
32	Spain	6.1	6	5.5 - 6.6
34	Dominica	5.9	3	4.9 - 6.7
35	Portugal	5.8	6	5.5 - 6.2
35	Puerto Rico	5.8	4	5.2 - 6.3
37	Botswana	5.6	6	5.1 - 6.3
37	Taiwan	5.6	9	5.4 - 5.9
39	Brunei Darussalam	5.5	4	4.7 - 6.4
39	Oman	5.5	5	4.4 - 6.5
39	Korea (South)	5.5	9	5.3 - 5.7
42	Mauritius	5.4	6	5.0 - 5.9
43	Costa Rica	5.3	5	4.7 - 5.9
43	Macau	5.3	3	3.3 - 6.9
45	Malta	5.2	4	4.0 - 6.2
46	Bahrain	5.1	5	4.2 - 5.8
46	Cape Verde	5.1	3	3.3 - 7.0
46	Hungary	5.1	8	4.6 - 5.7
49	Bhutan	5.0	4	4.3 - 5.6
49	Jordan	5.0	7	3.9 - 6.1
49	Poland	5.0	8	4.5 - 5.5

Rank	Country/Territory	CPI 2009 Score	Surveys Used	Confidence Range
52	Czech Republic	4.9	8	4.3 - 5.6
52	Lithuania	4.9	8	4.4 - 5.4
54	Seychelles	4.8	3	3.0 - 6.7
55	South Africa	4.7	8	4.3 - 4.9
56	Latvia	4.5	6	4.1 - 4.9
56	Malaysia	4.5	9	4.0 - 5.1
56	Namibia	4.5	6	3.9 - 5.1
56	Samoa	4.5	3	3.3 - 5.3
56	Slovakia	4.5	8	4.1 - 4.9
61	Cuba	4.4	3	3.5 - 5.1
61	Turkey	4.4	7	3.9 - 4.9
63	Italy	4.3	6	3.8 - 4.9
63	Saudi Arabia	4.3	5	3.1 - 5.3
65	Tunisia	4.2	6	3.0 - 5.5
66	Croatia	4.1	8	3.7 - 4.5
66	Georgia	4.1	7	3.4 - 4.7
66	Kuwait	4.1	5	3.2 - 5.1
69	Ghana	3.9	7	3.2 - 4.6
69	Montenegro	3.9	5	3.5 - 4.4
71	Bulgaria	3.8	8	3.2 - 4.5
71	FYR Macedonia	3.8	6	3.4 - 4.2
71	Greece	3.8	6	3.2 - 4.3
71	Romania	3.8	8	3.2 - 4.3
75	Brazil	3.7	7	3.3 - 4.3
75	Colombia	3.7	7	3.1 - 4.3
75	Peru	3.7	7	3.4 - 4.1
75	Suriname	3.7	3	3.0 - 4.7
79	Burkina Faso	3.6	7	2.8 - 4.4
79	China	3.6	9	3.0 - 4.2
79	Swaziland	3.6	3	3.0 - 4.7
79	Trinidad and Tobago	3.6	4	3.0 - 4.3
83	Serbia	3.5	6	3.3 - 3.9
84	El Salvador	3.4	5	3.0 - 3.8
84	Guatemala	3.4	5	3.0 - 3.9

Rank	Country/Territory	CPI 2009 Score	Surveys Used	Confidence Range
84	India	3.4	10	3.2 - 3.6
84	Panama	3.4	5	3.1 - 3.7
84	Thailand	3.4	9	3.0 - 3.8
89	Lesotho	3.3	6	2.8 - 3.8
89	Malawi	3.3	7	2.7 - 3.9
89	Mexico	3.3	7	3.2 - 3.5
89	Moldova	3.3	6	2.7 - 4.0
89	Morocco	3.3	6	2.8 - 3.9
89	Rwanda	3.3	4	2.9 - 3.7
95	Albania	3.2	6	3.0 - 3.3
95	Vanuatu	3.2	3	2.3 - 4.7
97	Liberia	3.1	3	1.9 - 3.8
97	Sri Lanka	3.1	7	2.8 - 3.4
99	Bosnia and Herzegovina	3.0	7	2.6 - 3.4
99	Dominican Republic	3.0	5	2.9 - 3.2
99	Jamaica	3.0	5	2.8 - 3.3
99	Madagascar	3.0	7	2.8 - 3.2
99	Senegal	3.0	7	2.5 - 3.6
99	Tonga	3.0	3	2.6 - 3.3
99	Zambia	3.0	7	2.8 - 3.2
106	Argentina	2.9	7	2.6 - 3.1
106	Benin	2.9	6	2.3 - 3.4
106	Gabon	2.9	3	2.6 - 3.1
106	Gambia	2.9	5	1.6 - 4.0
106	Niger	2.9	5	2.7 - 3.0
111	Algeria	2.8	6	2.5 - 3.1
111	Djibouti	2.8	4	2.3 - 3.2
111	Egypt	2.8	6	2.6 - 3.1
111	Indonesia	2.8	9	2.4 - 3.2
111	Kiribati	2.8	3	2.3 - 3.3
111	Mali	2.8	6	2.4 - 3.2
111	Sao Tome and Principe	2.8	3	2.4 - 3.3

Rank	Country/Territory	CPI 2009 Score	Surveys Used	Confidence Range
111	Solomon Islands	2.8	3	2.3 - 3.3
111	Togo	2.8	5	1.9 - 3.9
120	Armenia	2.7	7	2.6 - 2.8
120	Bolivia	2.7	6	2.4 - 3.1
120	Ethiopia	2.7	7	2.4 - 2.9
120	Kazakhstan	2.7	7	2.1 - 3.3
120	Mongolia	2.7	7	2.4 - 3.0
120	Vietnam	2.7	9	2.4 - 3.1
126	Eritrea	2.6	4	1.6 - 3.8
126	Guyana	2.6	4	2.5 - 2.7
126	Syria	2.6	5	2.2 - 2.9
126	Tanzania	2.6	7	2.4 - 2.9
130	Honduras	2.5	6	2.2 - 2.8
130	Lebanon	2.5	3	1.9 - 3.1
130	Libya	2.5	6	2.2 - 2.8
130	Maldives	2.5	4	1.8 - 3.2
130	Mauritania	2.5	7	2.0 - 3.3
130	Mozambique	2.5	7	2.3 - 2.8
130	Nicaragua	2.5	6	2.3 - 2.7
130	Nigeria	2.5	7	2.2 - 2.7
130	Uganda	2.5	7	2.1 - 2.8
139	Bangladesh	2.4	7	2.0 - 2.8
139	Belarus	2.4	4	2.0 - 2.8
139	Pakistan	2.4	7	2.1 - 2.7
139	Philippines	2.4	9	2.1 - 2.7
143	Azerbaijan	2.3	7	2.0 - 2.6
143	Comoros	2.3	3	1.6 - 3.3
143	Nepal	2.3	6	2.0 - 2.6
146	Cameroon	2.2	7	1.9 - 2.6
146	Ecuador	2.2	5	2.0 - 2.5
146	Kenya	2.2	7	1.9 - 2.5
146	Russia	2.2	8	1.9 - 2.4
146	Sierra Leone	2.2	5	1.9 - 2.4
146	Timor-Leste	2.2	5	1.8 - 2.6

Rank	Country/Territory	CPI 2009 Score	Surveys Used	Confidence Range
146	Ukraine	2.2	8	2.0 - 2.6
146	Zimbabwe	2.2	7	1.7 - 2.8
154	Côte d'Ivoire	2.1	7	1.8 - 2.4
154	Papua New Guinea	2.1	5	1.7 - 2.5
154	Paraguay	2.1	5	1.7 - 2.5
154	Yemen	2.1	4	1.6 - 2.5
158	Cambodia	2.0	8	1.8 - 2.2
158	Central African Republic	2.0	4	1.9 - 2.2
158	Laos	2.0	4	1.6 - 2.6
158	Tajikistan	2.0	8	1.6 - 2.5
162	Angola	1.9	5	1.8 - 1.9
162	Congo Brazzaville	1.9	5	1.6 - 2.1
162	Democratic Republic of Congo	1.9	5	1.7 - 2.1
162	Guinea-Bissau	1.9	3	1.8 - 2.0
162	Kyrgyzstan	1.9	7	1.8 - 2.1
162	Venezuela	1.9	7	1.8 - 2.0
168	Burundi	1.8	6	1.6 - 2.0
168	Equatorial Guinea	1.8	3	1.6 - 1.9
168	Guinea	1.8	5	1.7 - 1.8
168	Haiti	1.8	3	1.4 - 2.3
168	Iran	1.8	3	1.7 - 1.9
168	Turkmenistan	1.8	4	1.7 - 1.9
174	Uzbekistan	1.7	6	1.5 - 1.8
175	Chad	1.6	6	1.5 - 1.7
176	Iraq	1.5	3	1.2 - 1.8
176	Sudan	1.5	5	1.4 - 1.7
178	Myanmar	1.4	3	0.9 - 1.8
179	Afghanistan	1.3	4	1.0 - 1.5
180	Somalia	1.1	3	0.9 - 1.4

http://www.transparency.org/policy_research/surveys_indices/cpi/2009/
cpi_2009_table

Lightning Source UK Ltd.
Milton Keynes UK
29 September 2010

160538UK00009B/25/P